THE LEGACY OF YOUTH MINISTRY
& ITS EMERGENCE INTO THE 21ST CENTURY

VOLUME I

BY PAMELA MCNEESE

The Legacy of Youth Ministry & Its Emergence Into the 21st Century
ISBN: 978-1939570-65-9

Published by Word and Spirit Publishing
P.O. Box 701403
Tulsa, Oklahoma 74170
wordandspiritpublishing.com

TABLE OF CONTENTS

Preface

Over two decades ago, I was in one of the Bible schools that I attended. They had presentations to help students decide which area of concentration they would enter for study and training during their final year of ministerial training. I had no idea back then how one act of obedience would lead me down this path to complete this research that is so dear to my heart. It was during that time that the Holy Spirit impressed upon my spirit to enter into "Effective Youth Pastoring."

Many years later, when I entered the doctorate program, another decision had to be made regarding what my doctoral thesis would be. After some deliberation, the decision was made to research the history of youth ministry. The work of Volume 1 is the result of that decision. My understanding continues to ring ever clear regarding one act of obedience that triggered a chain of events in the plan of God and what God can do with it.

This work has brought back so many memories of how my own early youth biblical training transpired. Even though this has come in many forms and methods, the goal was the same from the beginning: "How shall a young man cleanse his way—by taking heed to Thy Word?" Who can fathom the mind of God, for His thoughts are far higher than ours? There is a profound responsibility given to those who would be and will be prevailed upon to share the future as God gave from the beginning to impact every generation.

The realization of our Judeo-Christian roots can never be eviscerated, nor the eternal truths that have been provided and made available concerning the revelation knowledge of God to every dispensation.

My desire for this work is to provide a brief insight into where it all began from Him "who knows the end from the beginning" as it relates to the "History of Youth Ministry and its Emergence into the Twenty-first Century." I hope that you will be blessed as I was.

Acknowledgements:

My honor and praise and gratitude to the Father God and to Jesus My Lord and Savior who, by His grace, called me by His Spirit from the seed of my father and my mother's womb and placed me in the earth realm for such a time as this!

Special thanks to the many Bible schools that I had the honor of attending!

Special thanks to the denominational church setting that God used to impart the foundation of holiness, hunger and the desire for God that was inflamed inside of my innermost being as a youth!

I wish to give thanks to all the pastors whom I have been blessed to be under and to every Bible teacher whom God has used to teach me the Word!

Very special thanks to my Editor, Dr. Gloria Collier, whose editorial excellence was a major contribution in completing this effort!

Finally, special thanks to my family!

INTRODUCTION

The purpose of this book is to communicate a concise overview of the origin and evolutionary legacy of youth ministry, and its emergence into the 21st century. The intended objective is to display how care for troubled youth impacted generations of youth and to explore the role of youth ministry in modern day culture and beyond.

Rearing teenage youth in these last days is a challenge for most parents. However, it does not have to be an issue when parents consistently apply the Word of God as it relates to children. God has not changed His Word, but the world has changed its ways. The world's ways and policies have changed in order to produce a culture that is against the God of the Bible and intolerant of His eternal truths that we were commanded to live by. Parents must not allow this to be a distraction or to persuade them to change their ways or views on what God speaks concerning children.

It will take hard work, discipline, patience, love, chastisement, peace, and a lot of prayer to get the truth into this generation that which will produce and manifest the character of holiness in them forever. Parents have a very short span of time to instill the values of God in their children. "There is a path before each person that seems right, but it ends in death." It would be advisable to not allow your kids to embrace a culture that is sinking toward the abyss. Control every avenue while it is within your sphere to make sure that children are not being consumed by the liberal culture that is "anti-God" into them. There is a small but concise space of time that parents, guardians, etc. have to make a God imprint on youth. As children begin adolescence and even preschool, due to the time we currently live, we can limit the ability to guard what is heard. It is paramount that the foundation of God's Word is planted first in the sponge of their hearts. Communicate to your kids when they are young the first commandment, which is "To love the Lord thy God with all your passion and prayer and intelligence" (Matt 22:37-40 MSG). Parents are their children's first view of God and have been commissioned by Scripture to teach and train their children by precept and example to serve the Lord.

Let's examine the big picture. In this discourse there are situations where the laws of the land that were in direct conflict with the roadmap given by Scripture and proved to be a negative constituency demonstrating example resistance to what God had commanded for children and youth.. History and insight are given on previous events that took place to demonstrate how the Word of God innovatively shaped and reshaped the youth church, and the children's church, to reveal how it has emerged into what it is today. Nevertheless, in this brief historical account, do not lose the very essence of the subject at hand. This exposition is based on historical accounts, but it is also a personal product of biblical values and precepts and a confirmation and validation that those commands are evident in the twenty-first century as an eternal truth that raising children God's way is still the best way. My goal is that you take from this the very thing that it took to write and explain this course of study: that the Spirit of God will be able to operate in your desire to apply the influence that brings eternal results.

To live and raise children in the things of God—not back in the times we are about to read, but in the twenty-first century—during the last of the last days, will take a determined effort. Many children attest to the fact that their biblical upbringing has sustained them like a compass, even when they moved toward the wrong direction, and that it was the rudder that eventually pulled them back into sobriety and morality.

The reason why the Sunday school movement was continually expanding as people were dying off is because the Spirit of God was moving it, to keep it going so that it could touch the world—even the world today. It was moving in order to make sure that the ones who read of these previous events would not forget that children and youth are the future yet a principal part of what God wants to do now. They are the ones that are a part of this generation who are going to witness the coming of the Lord. If the Lord tarries in His coming, think of how critical it will be for this generation to be carriers of the baton to the next generation.

The Spirit of God was moving the Sunday school movement through different vessels, so that when these last of the last arrived, people would know to go back to the basics and review the beginning when things began to be clouded. We must redeem the times that we live in, and use every opportunity to raise a generation that is going to be used by God in a way that none of us that came before them have ever experienced. Bear in mind, this study is researched from the viewpoint of the law of God, which is the beginning and end of wisdom, not from the viewpoint of secular society or culture.

CHAPTER I:

THE HISTORY OF THE SABBATH SCHOOL MOVEMENT

To adequately explore and to provide conclusive and accurate proof of the history of youth ministry, it is vital that we shed light on the history of the Sabbath School Movement and its origin. Many pioneers worked tirelessly and were used to pave the way for Christian education and instruction for all youth, independent of their social class.

The Jewish culture can be given the credit for educating children, women and strangers systematically with biblical and social education based on the commandment of God and the Scripture. This divinely authorized premise of Scripture for educating children naturally, socially, and spiritually was given multiple times in several different Scriptures, beginning with the commandments given by God to Moses in the book of Deuteronomy 31:11-13, which gave the commandment for all Israelites to come and appear before the Lord at a designated place that He chose. They were commanded to read the law in front of all the people of Israel for their hearing.[1] They were told to assemble the people—men, women, children and the stranger who traveled with them so that they too could learn reverence for the Lord. They were instructed to be watchful to do all the words of the law, so that the children who previously did not know the law of God would also learn the law of God so that a reverential fear would be instilled within them.

The Bible gives us the mandate for training up the children in the way that is right so that all the children will be taught the ways of the Lord and experience the peace that it provides, which cannot be obtained through material gain alone.

The Sabbath – Shabbat

- The people of Israel were commanded by God to gather together on the Sabbath day. The book of Exodus 20:8 states, "Remember the Sabbath Day by keeping it holy." Exodus 31:12-13 commanded Moses to speak to the people regarding maintaining the Sabbaths as a sign between God and them throughout generations that they would know that He was the Lord that doth sanctify them. This was, so that they would have moeds (appointed times with Him). The Sabbath was considered holy to God and was to be regarded as such to the Hebrew people as well, with the penalty of death for anyone who desecrated it under the dispensation of the law. Sabbath was to be a day of rest, holy to the LORD.[1] The Israelites are to observe the Sabbath, celebrating it for the generations to come as a lasting covenant." It was really a prototype that was designed to cause the people, as I like to say, to "make time for God." If you don't plan to schedule and make time for

God, an adversary will definitely work to fill that time with something else.

In Hebrew, the word "Shabbat" is the word for Sabbath, which is the seventh day of the Jewish week and a day of rest and worship. The Sabbath was also a time of reflection, remembrance, rehearsal, and instruction of the Holy Scriptures and the commandments of God as declared in the Torah and the Mishnah. The New Testament further solidifies the instructions on the Sabbath day in St. Luke 4:16-17, where it states that Jesus Himself went to Nazareth, where He grew up, and performed the customary practice of going into the synagogue on the Jewish day of Shabbat—reading from the Holy Scriptures, probably the Torah.

At the age of twelve, Jesus was found in the Jewish temple or synagogue conversing with the teachers. This is an evident sign that demonstrates the spiritual growth of the Messiah and validates the Scriptures that states He grew in wisdom and stature with God and with man.

The Jews had a systematic reading schedule for reading the Scriptures every Sabbath to adequately cover all the Torah, Law, Prophets and the Psalms within a three year cycle. There were many examples of Jesus going into the synagogue on the Sabbath day to preach, teach, and he also healed on the Sabbath Day. The Book of the Acts of the Apostles documents the ascension of Jesus to heaven and records the Apostles following His example. This was the Judeo practice and custom to enter the synagogues on the Sabbath day to preach and teach what the Scriptures had prophesied and point out

---

[1] Exodus 20:8

what the Torah had told their forefathers had been fulfilled in Jesus, the Messiah.

Early Judean Christian Education

The institution of early Biblical education can be attributed to the Jewish culture clearly as stated above in Scriptures from Exodus. History validates that every synagogue was a school and all the children were required to attend the schools on the Sabbath to receive that instruction. The history of formal education in ancient Israel and Judah dates as far back as 1300 BCE.[2]

However, the prophet Ezra was accredited with its origination in 459 BCE. It was said that Ezra, along with the help of the General Assembly, engineered the provision of public schools in Jerusalem, ensuring the education of fatherless adolescent boys over sixteen years of age. An institution known as the 'be rav" or "bet rabban" (house of teacher) was the blueprint for the formal school system, which actually evolved sometime later. A high priest by the name of Joshua Ben Gamla (64 CE), was instrumental in establishing this system. This development caused public schools systems to be opened in every town and included the enrollment of all children through ages six or above.

Torah commanded that education be provided to the entire society[2]. This commandment varied differently from other ancient civilizations that limited education to the elite classes of society or to those who aspired to be professional scribes. Education requires teaching and learning specific skills, and, more importantly, the

---

[2] http://en.wikipedia.org/wiki/History_of_education_in_ancient_Israel_and_Judah

transfer of knowledge along with a clear judgment and well-developed wisdom.

The synagogues were the germ for the early "Sabbath Schools," although they were not called "Sabbath Schools" in name, but were certainly established in principle. The Sabbath referred to here would have been the Jewish Sabbath (Friday from 6pm to Saturday 6pm) and not the Christian Sabbath (Sunday).

We must remember the Jewish culture and traditions that were in practice during the time in which our Lord and Savior Jesus Christ, a Jew, came into the world. Entire cultures are inevitably lost, unless the culture is passed down through generations. Neither the archives of history, nor the scribes, have been able to provide the world with the records on the life of Jesus after His birth and prior to age thirty. One of the few exceptions to this is when Jesus was twelve. The Scriptures clearly state that the parents of Jesus found Him in the synagogue, where He had transitioned from scholar to teacher.

The Sabbath Schools curriculum were instrumental in the continuing and successful implementation of the Torah teaching and Bible curriculum. Since repetition teachings are always helpful in cementing truths into the hearts of hearers, instructions were duplicated many times, thus the command to read the Shema' two times a day and to talk about it in the morning and the evening. It was through these Torah commandments that the Jewish nation and culture was preserved thoroughly by way of synagogue schools held on the Sabbath. Not only was the culture preserved through the Sabbath Schools, but the lineage of the Messiah was maintained through documentation and preserved by way of the Holy Scriptures and taught in the synagogue teachings on the Sabbath. They presented to the world the Jewish Messiah.

As the Messiah came to us through the Jewish race, so did the seed of the Sabbath School and the main subject areas that are divided in the Mishna. There were six areas of concentration that included: Zeraim or (seeds), which dealt with agricultural laws and also prayer; Moed (appointed times or feasts), which included the study of the laws of Shabbat and the laws of the festivals; Nashim, which translates (women), but basically dealt with the laws of marriage and divorce; and amazingly Nezikin, which is the foundation of civil and criminal law and (holy things) or (Kodashim), which was sacrificial rites regarding the Temple and dietary laws regarding food. The final area was the Tohorot or (purities), which basically dealt with laws and rules of purification for the priest and for the family.[3]

Even unbelieving Jews today still observe the seven feasts of Israel as commanded by God in the book of Deuteronomy. The Old Testament Scriptures (Torah), teachings and observance of the feasts themselves are the very types and shadows of the Christ that some Jews both willfully and ignorantly rejected. (The Scriptures clearly stated that Jesus came first to His own people and His own received Him not.[4])

The idea of gathering children for religious instruction has deep historical roots, as has been evidenced within the Jewish culture. Hebrews considered children a blessing from God, and during Pre-Exilic times in early Hebrew history before the years 586/587B.C., parents assumed the primary responsibility for educating the children. The Hebrew people were considered nomads and the tribal leaders also were included in the role of pedagogy[5].

---

3 http://en.wikipedia.org/wiki/History_of_education_in_ancient_Israel_and_Judah

4 St. John 1:10-12

5 http://Bibleresources.americanBible.org/Bible-resources/Bible-resource-center/about-the-Bible/Bible`-history/education-ancient-israel.

There were two Jewish men who are remembered for their contribution to Jewish education: one being the brother of Queen Alexandria (she reigned in 78-69 B.C.), namely Simeon Ben-Shetach, and Joshua Ben-Gamala. Ben-Gamala was considered to have made elementary education a requirement. The second teachers were esteemed very highly due to their phenomenal teaching ability. This was sometimes regarded higher than the teaching of the parents.

Hebrew women did teach the children, initially and throughout time, but the primary teachers were married males, who were required to have high moral standards, preferably even higher than their academic resumes. They were not compensated for teaching[6].

They used repetition and memorization techniques to instill the principles within the children and youth. The children were taught how to read and write, arithmetic and to memorize Scriptures. The commitment to teaching the children the Scriptures caused them to obtain knowledge of their Mosaic heritage. Many teaching centers emerged in the Jewish communities.

The first deportation of the Hebrews to Babylon covered a period of seventy years of exile, but the energy to train the children and preserve the priesthood was not diminished, even while they were in exile. Due to disobedience, the Jews experienced what is known as the diaspora, or scattering, on more than one occasion.

The dispersion of the Jews allowed for the establishment of synagogues, which would have included the Sabbath Schools. The mandate to teach the following generations was something that the Jews took very seriously. Therefore, it is safe to assume, and there is

---

[6] http://Bibleresources.americanBible.org/Bible-resources/Bible-resource-center/about-the-Bible/Bible -history/education-ancient-Israel

proof, that Sabbath Schools were implemented in the countries where they migrated to throughout the world and that education would have taken place in the synagogues. In addition, we must not forget that the apostles themselves, all being Jewish, were also products of the synagogues, which in principle contained Sabbath Schools.

The Sabbath Schools and Christian instruction for all were destined to become a permanent institution and began with children the majority of the time. As we explore various early records of the establishment of Sabbath Schools and their dates and societies of origin, keep in mind the commitment to education prevailed because of pedagogy and the strong desire to train children and a nation to be holy before God.[7]

The term "Sabbath School" began to refer to an establishment and creation of Sabbath Schools primarily and altogether as a separate entity from the synagogue as well. The Sabbath Schools' emergence has had a consistent impact on the world, which God used to educate children, youth and adults on the requirements of holy living, conduct and faith. This movement, a key predecessor to the Christian faith, continued to spread globally.

Christian Society – Catechumens

Christian instruction of the Scriptures, on Sundays specifically, usually began primarily with the youth of all ages, further validating and affirming the need for the Sabbath Schools. Interestingly enough, every primitive Christian society implemented some form of catechumens, which by definition is an ecclesiastical term meaning "one

---

7 Bible/Bible-history/education-ancient-Israel

receiving instructions from a catechist in the principles of Christian Religion and the view of baptism" as practiced by Christ and His apostles. This primarily consisted of Christian families and their children who were eager to receive instruction on the basic foundational doctrines of the Bible. During this time of catechumens, diverse groups met on Sundays and were taught the fundamental Christian values based on Scripture by elders, pastors and other leaders[8].

From the Dark Ages to the period of the Reformation, the germination of the Sabbath Schools did not dissipate. In early 1527 A.D., there are records showing that during the period of Reformation, Martin Luther himself shocked what then was the "religious world" with the revelation that all could be saved and obtain redemption through faith in the finished work of Christ. The revelation that the Reformation divulged was a strong challenger to unscriptural, traditional and superstitious teachings being refuted and therefore discredited. Deceptive bonds were broken, and this brought understanding and relevant liberty to the Church of Christ.

Martin Luther adamantly and genuinely desired to share the knowledge he received. He seemed to have the sense that all would be lost if he failed to educate the children and young, which would eliminate and absolve them of scriptural ignorance through true Bible interpretation. Martin already knew from personal experience that "mental" education was not enough to satisfy the hunger that only faith and true worship could bring. He seemed to possess the moral obligation and passion to pass on what he received concerning salvation by faith and not by works. It seemed his intent was to preserve the knowledge of the revelation of scriptural truths he received.

---

[8] http://www.newadvent.org/cathen/13554b.htm

Martin Luther established religious instruction for children and youth on the Sabbath, ensuring that the morality and undeniable treasures of the teachings of Christ would continue to the next generations.

Martin Luther can be accredited with responsibility for the foundation that was laid for religious schools in Germany. The formats of these schools in Germany was like the early Sabbath school services and structure. They, too, were held on Sundays and were staunchly devoted to the concentration of Bible catechism, for times of songs of praise, and for placing great emphasis on prayer.

Germany thus acquired the institution and establishment of the Sabbath School, John Knox implemented the system of Sabbath School at the beginning of the Reformation. In addition, John Brown had a Sabbath School in the town of Priesthill in Scotland. (Jews were in Rome as early as the Second Century B.C. under the alliance of Judea's Maccabeus and during the time of Christ.) Although the Sabbath schools were in existence prior to the Second Century B.C. in Rome, it is possible that the advertisement of the schools was more among Jews due to the Jewish teachings and even their Messiah being a considerable threat to the Roman way of life.

The Synagogue a School – Early Global Sabbath Schools

Wherever the Jewish people settled and made their homes, there were synagogues in functional existence.

It would be hard to imagine that the practice of the Sabbath School was absent even in Rome, where Christians and Jews were heavily persecuted throughout history. An established presence of Jews already in Rome as well as those sent to Rome as slaves give a strong inclination that Sabbatical teachings and synagogue attendance, along with Sabbath Schools, would have been necessary and would have been a part of their culture and tradition.

Prior to the year of 1584, Charles, "Carlos" Borromeo of Milan, Italy, was a very young devoted Christian. His uncle, Pope Pius IV, apparently saw the visible evidence of a call of God on his nephew's life, and at the age of twelve, his uncle appointed him to the honorary role of abbot. Carlos Borromeo completed a doctorate degree before he turned twenty-five and was subsequently promoted to the title Archbishop of Milan. It was this archbishop, who had studied the civil and canon law at a very early age, who established Sabbath Schools in the Cathedral of Milan and then throughout his diocese, which covered the geographical area from Milan to Lombardy, Italy[9].

By the year of 1232, there was an established Jewish community in Ireland in the city of Dublin.[10] Persecution arose and indicates there were some expulsions of the Jews after this time, but regardless of the persecution and activities of the Diaspora, there was eventually a permanent residence of Jews established by the fifteenth century and a Jewish synagogue by the year 1660. This indicates that Ireland was not exempt from the Sabbatical School movement as well.

Additional evidence seems to support the fact that Scotland had schools of religious instruction since around 1560 A.D. It appears that the University Commissioners of Scotland noticed a neglect of the adherence and teaching to the foundations of the Christian Faith and encouraged all of the scholars to consider carefully the Sabbath day sermons and lessons that were included in the Catechism. Reverend

---

9 http://en.wikipedia.org/wiki/History_of_the_Jews_in_Italy

10 http://en.wikipedia.org/wiki/Arminianism

Jim Brown of Scotland documented the existence of Sabbath Schools in Glasgow and other areas of Scotland around the year 1707 A.D. Catholicism had been the universal religion with Protestant and Lutheran movements emerging around the time of the Reformation.

The Origin of the American Sabbath Schools

In the year of 1737, John Wesley, having traveled from England to Savannah, Georgia, established Sabbath Schools in America. He spent two years in Georgia, but after experiencing some issues there he returned to England. However, the Sabbath Schools themselves, continued under the guidance of his brother, Charles Wesley, and Reverend George Whitfield."

The town of Bethlehem, Connecticut, also boasted a Sabbath School in the year 1740, established by a Reverend Joseph Bellamy. He seemed to receive further light and more instruction on the format of the Sabbath Schools. He applied that knowledge, allowing the Sabbath School to thrive even more, and it continued indefinitely. By the beginning of the American Revolution, there also began the establishment of a Sabbath School in Ephrata, Lancaster County, Pennsylvania. It was established and led by a man by the name of Ludwig Strecker. The system of the Sabbath School was well in motion. John Knox received commendation for establishing Sabbath Schools at the beginning of the Reformation.

As the germination of the Sabbath Schools continued throughout America, we must give an account of the leaders of the movement, who not only started Sabbath Schools, but also paved the way for movement that God Himself ordained to bring His Word to all mankind by vehicle of the children and youth.

Chapter II

JOHN WESLEY: METHODISM AND SABBATH SCHOOL INSTITUTION

John Benjamin Wesley was born in Epworth, London on June 28th, 1703. He was the fifteenth child born to Samuel and Susannah Wesley. His father was a graduate of Oxford University and was also a minister of the Church of England. At the age of six, John Wesley was miraculously rescued from a burning rectory. The manner in which he was rescued made an indelible impression on his mind, and he spoke of himself as a "brand plucked from the burning" and had an inward knowing that he was indeed a child of Providence. John's mother, Susannah, educated John and all of his eighteen siblings very early. She was a woman of extreme intelligence and deep piety, gifted in teaching and a stern disciplinarian.

In the year of 1713, John was enrolled at Charterhouse School, London, where he began his collegiate studies. John followed his methodical, studious, and religious lifestyle at Charterhouse that his mother had taught him at home. His training for ministry occurred at Christ Church College in Oxford. By the age of twenty-three, he was ordained a deacon and served with his father as a curate for two years. He died at the age of eighty-eight on March 2, 1791.

Methodism and its founder helped in producing the early soil in which the Sunday schools, which began as the Sabbath Schools, were able to flourish, both in Europe and in America. A prayer and Bible study held in the home of John Wesley became the birth of the Wesleyan Church of England in the year 1738.

The Wesleys were a family of nineteen children, and Susannah Wesley felt the need to spend time with her children on Sunday evenings. Since there were no evening church services and her husband was absent due to a sentence to serve time in the debtor's prison for unpaid debts, she began to teach her children Bible lessons. They also sang songs. She was instrumental in laying a solid foundation in the Wesley's by reading prayers to them, reading sermons, and conversing with the children over other topics in her home. Therefore, it was the mother of John Wesley, Suzanne Wesley, who produced the product of the Wesley children and trained them for the ministry that was ordained for them, given with divine ability and grace.

Sunday was the designated day for Christian teachings, primarily for the purpose of religious instruction. This assisted and allowed a track record and practical preparation that influenced Methodism and some beginnings for the Sunday school of 1780. Suzanne Wesley can be credited for exemplary stamina and determination with excellent teaching skills as she knowingly implemented the plan of God with the foundation that was created in her children. God unquestionably and undeniably used Suzanne Wesley to sprout yet another germ of the Sabbath School in the teaching of her own children the moral truths and social habits of the Bible, which was clearly the mandate from God to Moses concerning the children of Israel. This was yet another, undeniable germ of the Sabbath School that God used to impact centuries of children and it initiated yet another movement.

The classes being taught by Mrs. Wesley in their house quickly grew to over two hundred children, and many other children were turned away for lack of room. The Wesley's were considered the cream of the crop, the elite, and belonged to a well-educated class of aristocrats in England. Despite all this the Wesley's themselves had the children of the poor in their own house in London and provided for them with food and clothing. Religion was the prominent aim, as was the enforcement of the principles of the faith and the Bible, as well as social and educational training, all free of charge. Suzanne Wesley was a perfect example of what the Scriptures meant when the Apostle Paul told Timothy, a young pastor: "Endure hardness as a good soldier of Jesus Christ." If Suzanne Wesley had thought she had too many children and no time to teach them the Word of God or because she was pregnant quite frequently and could not do it, the Methodist Church may not have been founded. Suzanne had marvelous and valid opportunities to make excuses as to why she should not teach and train her own children the Bible.

The Wesley's were also responsible for the implementation of an orphan house that was run by a new master and a woman teaching the fundamental principles of Christ, as well as general care for the children. This paved the way for Robert Raikes, a philanthropist of England, who years later saw the need to implant morality, educational and social skills that were privy to the rich in the minds of the youth and children. This laid the foundation for an explosion of immeasurable results that led to what has been called for more than two centuries as the "Sunday School."

John Wesley - Sabbath Schools in England

John Wesley's diary bares his thoughts regarding the establishment of preacher's and pastor's ministry to children. He also engineered the pastoral guidelines and helpful suggestions for ministering to the children. Some of the preachers complained, giving the weak excuse of not having a gift for ministering to the children and youth. John Wesley was so adamant in this evangelism endeavor that it is reported he stated that if the preachers could not minister to children, then the validity of their claims to be called Methodist preachers was certainly questionable. Wesley had his share of challenges justifying religious education for youth in the churches he organized as he dealt with the preachers. He insisted that they practice and practice until they could do it successfully.

The Methodist Episcopalian church was responsible for over fifty years of the Sabbath Schools organizational structure, as John Wesley himself became the superintendent of the movement within the Methodist church specifically.

John Wesley had vision and proven methods that provided direction and answers to assist the pastors in ministering to the children. His instructions seemed very basic and effective in that he wanted every preacher to survey the towns for the children, to plan and prepare to minister to them on a level where they could understand, and to receive instructions on the things of God. He also communicated that he wanted them to be very gentle with the children and not to bruise their spirits with rashness and discourage them. He wanted the preachers to practice reciting with the children to determine if they were absorbing the teachings. He wanted them to eradicate any illiteracy of the Scripture and to teach them the foundational doctrines of Christ.

John Wesley considered the ministry to the children to be a matter of supreme importance and that it was the greatest part in the building for a wise master builder, being more important than the building. He suggested meeting with the children separate from adults at church, providing material simple enough for the children to grasp the truths of the Bible. Is it any wonder that Jesus said, "Suffer little children, and forbid them not, to come unto me: for of such is the kingdom of heaven"? (Matthew 19:14)

John Wesley even gave the instructions for making the ministering to the children very personal after instruction by taking them aside and carefully showing them their sins by leading them in the prayers of repentance and acceptance of Christ as their Savior, but making carefully sure that they understood what was happening to them. Along with the instruction for leaders, John Wesley himself had his own personal and wonderful results with his experiences with children and youth.

Georgia and the American Sabbath School

In a missionary journey to America in the year 1735, John Wesley visited Savannah, Georgia, where he taught the Indian and American children on Sunday. He became all things to those he preached to by identifying himself with the children. He went to his meetings barefoot to encourage the children who did not have shoes to come to the meeting. The small groups' strategy was a great success for John

Wesley at Count Zinzendorf at Herr Hut, where he again taught children religious instruction and saw more success in small groups of ten when he included both the children and adults. Wesley used the idea of the small groups plan when he implemented his new church.

Wesley had been in the habit of meeting children and ministering to them directly, and he kept a journal of his ministerial events. In 1756, he taught a class of one hundred children catechism twice a week and commented on his disappointment that the pastors were not doing it regularly. Wesley recorded in his diary that in 1758 he met to teach some children and did not have high expectations, but that soon changed when the children responded hungrily to the Word of God with crying and tears of repentance. For nearly thirty years, John Wesley held services or classes of religious instruction for children, which was of considerable help when establishing the Methodist Churches.

At this point, the Sabbath School in the Methodist church was being held on Sunday and had evolved basically to the name Sunday school.

It was through John Wesley's foundation at home and during his time at collegiate biblical studies that they begin to call the group that was associated with him "The Methodist Society" because of the method of biblical study, sacrifice, and sanctification in which they were determined to live and practice.

By the year of 1769, a Hannah Ball of the city of Wycombe opened yet another Sunday school for the purpose of training children in the Holy Scriptures. She wrote a letter to John Wesley describing her school. She indicated that she met twice a week on Sundays and Mondays. Hannah also indicated that her labor among the children was earnest in order to promote the cause of the Gospel and Church of our Lord Jesus Christ. One particular obituary of a deceased Mrs. Sophia Cooke—who married the Rev. Samuel Bradburn, and who was born in Gloucester, England—gave credit to her receiving salvation and the grace of God at the age of eighteen when she united herself with the Methodist Society. Her obituary documented that she had been a member of the Methodist Society until her death at the age of seventy-five.

It was this woman, who was a product of the Methodist Society founded by John Wesley at a very young age, who made the suggestion of the Sunday school method to Mr. Robert Raikes, the philanthropist, concerning the poor, neglected children of Gloucester. She suggested that they teach them to read and take them to church. She assisted him in the initial organization and was one of the first and most effective Sunday school teachers in Gloucester, England. As it stands, Methodism primarily gained its largest following and reception among the common people and seemed most effective among them.

As president and founder and superintendent of the Sunday school, John Wesley whole-heartedly committed all of his time to the work of the church and the extension of the Sunday school movement. Wesley was also the editor of one of the earliest periodicals known to the Protestant world, titled the "Armenian Magazine." The magazine's general idea held to the doctrine by Jacobus Armenians, whose beliefs held closely to those of Wesley. The Armenian's doctrine believed in salvation by faith, through grace and not by works and that atonement for sin was and is through Jesus Christ alone. Unlike Calvinism, they believed that man could reject the grace of God and could fall from that grace through unconfessed sin. They believed that man could either accept or reject salvation from God by an act of his own free will.

Sunday School Advertisement and Publicity

Wesley published the first volume in the year of 1778, but it was in the year of 1785 that he printed an article advertising the charitable Sunday School that was started by Robert Raikes at Gloucester. He also printed accounts in the periodical of the various charitable Sunday Schools that had sprung up in diverse areas of England. The paper was an invaluable tool, but it was not the cause for the Methodists engaging in and following his work in the Sunday schools. It was solely based on the personal integrity of John Wesley himself and the results that his work had brought. John Wesley's name preceded him as he went from society to society and established networking contacts within the Methodist churches where he personally preached and inspired others to follow the mandate of working with the children and youth. John Wesley's journals gives credence to the early Wesleyan Sunday school progress, and it continually charted the growth and emergence.

In the Armenian periodical, John Wesley described how in the year of 1784 he traveled to a church in Bingley, where he preached both Sunday morning and evening services.[11] During these he observed a Sunday school class of over two hundred children being taught by several teachers. He indicated receiving praise reports of the effects the Sunday school had produced in the children's morality and social skills. He recorded how, in all his travels, he saw the Sunday schools springing up and sprouting like grass. Wesley began to get a glimpse of what God had envisioned all along. He realized that possibly God may have had a deeper intention than what he himself had realized for the Sunday school.

---

[11] http://en.wikipedia.org/wiki/Arminianism

In another city where John traveled, he documented in April of 1786 on Easter Sunday in Warrenton that there was a house crowded with over five hundred and fifty children. It looked like an army as the children swarmed him during his visit. Yet another account gave the sum in Bolton of over eight hundred poor children being taught in Sunday schools in the Methodist church. The teachers were not paid but were serving and indicated that they looked for their reward in heaven.

It is also important to remember that among their many talents of evangelism, pastoral work, and missionary work, both John Wesley and his brother Charles were prolific writers of hymns. What better place to see the fruit and practice of hymns for worship other than among the children and youth and in the Sunday schools.

So apparent was that fruit from the hymns, as in the particular Sunday school in Bolton, that the children were taught to sing, and it appears that a youth choir was instituted along with the worship. John Wesley described their singing as so awesome that it rang with the sound and unity of one voice; the presence of God was so intense that the children were weeping and some of them could not continue singing. He likened the singing to that of angels in its sound and stressed that he did not believe such a sound was anywhere in the universe. He said the children and youth's voices united as if a heavenly host was present among them and that he had never before witnessed singing and voices sounding like angels worshiping God in heaven.

His travels increased to many others cities; where they advertised his coming to town, the crowds increased dramatically. In April of 1788, the Sunday school John Wesley visited in Chester, England, had over a thousand children. The children were clean and appeared so well behaved and orderly. They, too, had a choir, and they sang with the melody so beautiful that it surpassed that of a symphony. These youth had the practice of visiting other youths in small groups to sing, comfort and pray with them, and true discipleship was clearly demonstrated and evident among them.

Two of the letters written by Wesley shortly before his location changed from earth to heaven were commending some of those ministers and preachers that were a product of his ministry at their local Sunday school chapters in the city where the Monkwearmouth church was located. The Sunday school was of such an excellence that on Sunday, the streets were cleared out of the poor children. He addressed a Reverend Duncan Wright with compliments on the quality and integrity of the Sunday school in his area for the poor children. He also wrote to the minister at Newcastle, which had several hundred children present weekly in the Sunday school. None of the teachers were paid a salary but volunteered out of their Christian duty and a heart for the things of God and the children.

The efforts of the Methodist Sunday school in 1812 represented about sixty thousand children instructed weekly in Great Britain alone.

Major growth was recognized in the year of 1860, totaling 474,900 in attendances in the Sunday Schools.

By the year, 1790, the majority of the clergy were Methodist and the people of the towns contributed generously with their finances in support of the Sunday schools. They showed preference to the Methodist church in their support, mainly because of the success of the Sunday school and its definite impact upon the younger generation. The rise and progress of Sunday schools in England, which originated from Sabbath Schools, were definitely not isolated cases, nor was John Wesley the only person who sensed a mandate to educate the lower classes of the children and youth biblically, socially, and morally.

In 1786, Reverend John Fletcher sensed an urgency to help and assist the poor children and the uninstructed children. He had his own school where he taught every day. However, when he heard about the success of the Methodist Sunday school, he changed his school and adopted the Sunday school method with a sizeable beginning of about three hundred children. He instructed the children until his death and wrote a paper called "The Advantages Likely to Arise from Sunday Schools."

John Lancaster founded the London Road Wesleyan Sunday School inside of a cellar in the city of Manchester, England. As his Sunday school grew quickly, he soon had a room built especially just for the Sunday school.

Another friend of Wesley, Cornelius Bayley, a master of a Kingswood School, was now an ordained minister in Manchester who published a public address to the Sunday school, encouraging other cities to follow the example in their neighborhoods. Reverend Richard Rodda was a personal friend and a protégé of Wesley, having been a member of the Methodist Society. He formed a Sunday school in Chester, England, with the help of some of the leading members of the society. In Chester, the Sunday school was one of the largest schools, and he made known the pure motives of the teachers who strictly did it for the good of the next generation.

The Sunday School movement expanded here and also focused on visitation and instruction of people in their homes. The concern was about the future of the generations to come and the determination of the movement to have results that were lasting. They came to the realization that the movement would only last a generation if they did not do something to plan for it to be imparted to future generations. The Bible records examples of generations that "knew not the Lord, nor what He had done." This is referring generations that coexist, but one supersedes the other, because has not been taught the history of their past. In modern vernacular, some call it Generation X. The X Generation is simply a progeny of people that do not fear God and have not been taught the things of God.

Another person who contributed to the history of the Sunday school movement was William Marriott, who was also one of the early Methodist leaders. At the age of twenty-one he devoted all his spare time to the promotion of Sunday schools. With his own money, he built the first Sunday school building in London, England, Friar's Mount, Bethel Green. He is accredited with the compilation of the Sunday School Union.

Marriott was one of the first to prepare and publish textbooks for devotional reading for every day in the calendar year. The title was "Plan for the Regulation of Sunday Schools" and was widely circulated. He engineered the publication of the first magazine for adolescents for ten years titled "The Youths Magazine," which was used by many as the primary guide of religious periodicals for young people.

Just like the Sabbath Schools, Methodism spread to Ireland, and they were very quick to respond to the Sunday school idea. Leaders in Ireland made it publicly known that it was their desire that Sunday schools and their societies be established as far as possible in all the towns of Ireland by the year 1794.

After the death of John Wesley in 1790, the movement of the Sunday school in the Methodist church did not diminish. As Methodism grew, so did the Sunday school society. Legislation in England was passed which would be a possible role model for the

American Methodist church. There was a need for activities that would further enhance the Sunday School Society and an organizational system to meet the problems that were surfacing.

In the year 1798, a Methodist Sunday School Society was established in Chapel, London. Doctor Coke and Doctor Whitehead were the first to preach at the Society conference where prominence was given to the Sunday schools. More structure was provided and the plan. Much like the Jewish requirements for a synagogue, the plan was that wherever there were ten children in a Society they would meet with them for one hour every week and to visit them at home as well as praying earnestly for them and instructing their parents. The path to the parents seemed to lead through the children and the path to the children was through the parents. The structure insisted that every possibility be exhausted to make sure that the plan was successful in planting the Sabbath seed in the present generation and for generations to come.

The initial Sunday school movement focused on children, and eventually adults too, who were both illiterate and poor. However, as it emerged, the emphasis became more on religious instruction only. The goal was to remove the burden of teaching secular subjects such as reading and writing from the instructors and to focus more on the great commission of Christ in the Gospels. This brought about a change in the Sunday school legislation.

Relations to Religious Education

The legislation aimed to change the efforts from education to salvation. All managers and teachers were impressed upon to make the salvation of the children their object in the Sunday school institution, and this was a very decided distinction. This also placed the responsibility back on the parents, which was the commandment of God for the parents to teach the children and reinforce what the children received in Sunday school, making a more indelible impression.

In 1748, the preachers were directed to place the children in "societies" for "suitable exhortations." In 1766, publications were created for the religious instruction and training of children. Between the years of 1784 to 1797, the focus was placed on the parents enforcing the religious instruction in the homes and Sunday school classes being formed for the poor children. In 1798, the establishment of the Methodist Sunday School Society was officially formed.

By the year 1805, the work of the Sunday school was generously supported financially and flourishing tremendously.

By the year 1808, by all accounts the Sunday school was carefully linked to the church; the pastor was required to be a part of the Sunday school committee. He was required to insist upon the attendance of the children in the regular church services as well. A conference in 1817 insisted upon the continued effort of teachers and children attending church services. In the year 1823, the urgency of only catechetical and religious instruction was recommended. Although the initial motive of the Sunday school movement was education and biblical education, the move had retreated back to the original plan of God for the Sabbath, with Bible teaching and worship being the only emphasis. God's commandment to honor the Sabbath and keep it holy was standing strong here.

In John Wesley's journals, he reports numbers in the one thousands when he traveled to the various cities to visit Methodist churches as the Sunday school superintendent and as the founder of Methodism. After thirty years, the numbers of scholars or children instructed by the Methodists in Great Britain had risen to over sixty thousand children. The Sunday school movement encompassed both British and foreign Bible societies.

A Calvinistic Methodist preacher by the name of Reverend Thomas Charles, of Bala, instituted the Sunday school society in the country of Wales. According to Mr. J. A. James, the Sunday school education in Wales increased so dramatically that the Welsh Bible supply in the country was depleted. As a result, Reverend Thomas Charles traveled to London to secure funding for the printing of a new edition of the Bible. The Religious Tract Society came up with the idea to furnish the whole world with the Word of God[12]. The idea was embraced and plans began immediately to make the blessing that came to them from the opportunity of the Welsh reprint. In actually, the impetus had originated from the Throne of God for them to undertake the task, and He provided the financing.

Wesleyan missionaries also established Sunday schools in Asia on the Island of Ceylon, not far from the British Empire. The Methodist Wesleyan missionaries traveled to all quarters of the Asian empire of Ceylon to establish Sunday schools. The missionaries faced obstacles but prevailed and reaped a harvest of more than two hundred and fifty children and at least twenty teachers. They provided instruction every week.

The Reverend Joseph Alleine had a Sabbath School in connection with his church at Taunton, Somersetshire, England. In 1767, the Reverend John Frederick Oberlin established the first "infant school," better known as "children's church." He required the children from the five surrounding villages that composed his parish to attend the

---

[12] http://en.wikipedia.org/wiki/Thomas_Charles

parish church, and he established a rotation every Sabbath. The service consisted of singing hymns and reciting lessons they had committed to memory during the week. The order of service for the Sabbath schools also included the pastor speaking a sermon message for all in attendance. Another Sabbath School was started even in the foreign land of Bohemia.

Chapter III

THE ROBERT RAIKES SUNDAY SCHOOL MOVEMENT

The germination of the seed of the Sabbath Schools continued to grow and proved to be unstoppable around the world. Many great men and women, especially John Wesley, should be accredited with the birth of the Sunday school movement, particularly in England, but it was purportedly Robert Raikes' ingenuity and expertise that brought it to the forefront in England with his plan that actually encompassed education and Christian education. What is important to understand about the Robert Raikes movement is that the focus was primarily on the poor and the eradication of illiteracy along with provisions to eliminate the element of bad character in the undisciplined youths that had become somewhat of menaces to society.

Mr. Robert Raikes was born in Gloucester, England, on September 14, 1736. He attended the University of Cambridge, but he did not matriculate. Having opted out of college, he chose to pursue a hands-on approach with the family publishing business instead. His father was the printer and the publisher of a newspaper called the *Gloucester Journal.* At the age of twenty-one, Robert's father died and Robert succeeded him in the publication of the *Journal's*[13].

The journal was used basically for political and religious information and marketing more than for its profitability. Since Robert's family fortune was considerable, he did not have to be concerned with earning a living. This afforded him the opportunity to engage wholeheartedly and liberally to use the the paper for the use of the work of the Kingdom of God. Robert Raikes was the sole proprietor of the only printing press in several countries for many years.

The Prophet of the Sunday School

Robert Raikes was given the title, "Father of the Sunday School" because he was viewed as the "prophet" of the Sunday school. Robert advertised the Sabbath school in the *Gloucester Journal,* which was edited by John Wesley.

Many great men and women were noted because of their individual contribution of Sabbath Schools or Sunday Schools for children. These trailblazers and their contributions to the movement should be widely known and acclaimed. However, some believe Borromeo, Alleine, the Wesleys and others in Europe, and others in America have not received adequate recognition for their accomplishments and contributions in instituting the Sabbath School or in the Sunday School Movement. The reason for this was that many people had the perception that some of the leaders' contributions to the movement

---

[13] Power, Carroll, John. *The Rise and Progress of the Sunday School.* Robert, Raikes and William Fox. New York. Sheldon and Company, 1863

were not systematic enough to maintain and perpetuate the same level of germination after the individual leaders died, causing the movements to suffer abrupt malfunctions.

Child Labor and the Industrial Revolution

The Industrial Revolution began in England around the year of 1733, a few years before Robert Raikes was born. The Industrial Revolution began the automation of the modern world, beginning with England, but it also had severe negative consequences that came with it. The schedule of the children and youth Sunday school had to be coordinated on Sunday only, due to the explosion of Industrial Revolution.

Many factory owners were in need of cheap, unskilled labor, and they profited greatly by using children and women as machine operators. Children as young as six years of age were expected to work up to fourteen hours a day in factories. It was not the automation but the ill of requiring the children and youth to work excessively grueling and laborious jobs that proved to be a very misguided side effect with significantly dire consequences. Many of the children sickened and died from working around the toxic fumes, and others were badly injured and sometimes killed while working in environments that were dangerous and unsafe. It was mainly the poor and uneducated children and youths that were made upon to work the grueling hours and days of labor, as they had no other means of survival. They were left alone on Sundays to fend for themselves, and they became menaces to the societies around them.

England saw crime and illiteracy among the youth escalating, but Robert Raikes had a plan. Mr. Raikes had surpassed all the leaders of the Sunday school movement that preceded him in supplying books to the movement. However, because he left a system of supply after his death, a plan for the future generations, and continuance of what he had begun also contributed to him being remembered as the Father of the Sunday School.

Methodism was an exception, but it seemed that when some leaders of the individual movements passed away, the work they had established did not continue with the same tenacity. Mr. Robert Raikes' family background and history was associated with honorable positions in the society throughout England for several centuries. The success of the Robert Raikes Sunday school organization is also closely associated with Methodism, and along with his own unselfish character, it helped to make it a success.

Ministry to the Incarcerated

Diversity played a key role in connections and networking was broadened as a result of the many different classes of people, presumably throughout the entire country of England. Robert Raikes' networking capabilities and his connections to the elite allowed him certain advantages regarding the Sunday school work.

Mr. Raikes' first benevolent mission was called the "Raikes Ragged School." It was given the name because Raikes was the leader of a committee that was instrumental in aiding men that were sent to prison. He gained the reputation and was initially described as someone who helped the poor. He used the ink of his newspapers, his personal influence, and his own property to help facilitate the procurement of basic humane conditions for those who were incarcerated.

The prisons at the time were in such inhumane and deplorable conditions that Robert seemed to focus his attention on the poor debtors there first. He aimed to make conditions more suitable for the prisoners, and he searched for a woman of character who could instruct them in religious instruction. They had no way of really acquiring food and the basic essentials needed. So, along with food, he made available to them moral and religious instruction by encouraging those prisoners who were able to read in various ways. He began with assembling some of the prisoners together for the teacher to teach them. The religious and moral instruction guide was the Bible and Christian literature. He saw such improvement in the prisoners that he determined to persevere and proceed with implementing an inside work designed for prisoners to keep their minds occupied.

Raikes was also instrumental in assisting, developing, and supporting the in house prison reform system for the inmates. For a period of some years, Raikes really focused on those youth and adults that were incarcerated who were paying debts to society. His efforts were mostly for rehabilitation educationally, socially, and morally. He seemed convinced that if he eliminated the ignorance of the individuals who perpetuated the crimes against society by providing books for educating them and Christians books and Bibles for moral character renewal, as well as spiritual knowledge, it would drastically affect them in a positive way.

The Industrial Revolution was moving ahead at full speed, and child labor was still a huge factor that contributed to the idleness and the blatant exploitation of the children who had nowhere to go on Sundays. Sunday was the only day that they were not required to work, and it was the day they seemed to be left completely idle and prone to mischief. Raikes was not blind to this. When he was in a certain neighborhood with the plan of employing a gardener to work for him, he was appalled by the behavior of the young boys and girls and realized that idleness was part of the problem. Raikes was convinced that crime was the direct result of poverty and ignorance. While the Industrial Revolution had a huge positive side, it also directly contributed to the problem.

As with any endeavor that involves remolding character, some results are forthcoming and some are disappointing. He felt that if he could possibly transform the behavior of the young and the adults and eliminate idleness and ignorance at an early age that he could prevent the cycle from perpetuating and hopefully thwart many from becoming the menaces to society that so many had already become. Raikes had the idea to try by starting with the children that he witnessed on the streets on Sundays. He was willing to use his idea in an experiment for three years to determine if his plan would work.

It was in the year of 1780 that he first gathered boys and paid a poor woman a schilling to teach them the Bible and Scriptures. Raikes himself also began to teach them reading and writing. This he did for a period of three years with very satisfactory results, but he did not advertise it at this time. His business associates thought that he had possibly gone mad when they saw him gathering mobs of poverty-stricken children from their neighborhoods every Sunday and leading them to the Raikes School. He promised them candy and coins just to sit still and listen, and the children came. The teachers read to them the Scriptures and simple stories regarding morality. Raikes hired three more teachers.

It was during these first three years of the Raikes Ragged School that he defied the normal traditions and combined the sexes in the classes every Sunday morning. Although most of the children were from the poor neighborhoods, there were some from even more prevalently slum neighborhoods who could not attend the Raikes School, so he brought the school to them on Sunday by way of the literature he printed, which included the alphabet and verses from the Bible on it. The attendance at the Raikes Ragged School saw tremendous growth.

The Prototype and the Explosion

The Raikes Ragged School was his prototype for research and development of a system that he planned on implementing based on the results. This was the Raikes Sunday school plan that stood out; he is definitely remembered for it. This revival of the Sunday school under Robert Raikes initially started with three derivatives: paying teachers for the instructions, instruction of the basics such as reading and spelling (other schools later modified these two features). The third feature that the Raikes School was characterized by limiting the teachings to children from the lower class.

It was during this time that Wesley wrote of the Raikes Sunday School movement in his editorial entitled "*the Armenian.*" Raikes supervised an experiment that showed promising results if followed, and due to its success, Raikes was convinced that he had the plan that would prove effective for everyone. He called it "The Sunday School Movement." The Sunday School Movement was officially birthed on November 3, 1783. He published it in his newspaper and began regular weekly advertising of the movement. He also used another journal called the *Gentleman's Magazine* for announcements of the Sunday School. Five schools were established within one year of the official launching of the movement.

Raikes orchestrated the organization of the schools by setting up rules and putting a management structure into place through a board. Raikes used the Gloucester newspaper he owned as a great source of communication, advertising, and constant exposure. He was able to garner considerable help from men of great character and wealth as well as other valuable resources such as John Wesley and Reverend George Whitfield. He was the author and publisher of textbooks for the schools, which were prepared specifically to address the problem of literacy such as *Redinmadesy* (reading made easy). The contents were in total harmony with the intentions of the Sunday school goals, and the assignment was to furnish opportunity and instructions to the poor children without interrupting their weekly work schedules.

The germ of the Sunday School Movement had flourished and exploded within four years after the official birth. The total number of students had increased to 250,000; in the city of Newcastle alone, there were five thousand pupils.

The Robert Raikes' system was widely known and accepted as a deterrent for the demoralization of a generation of children and youth. His results were divinely phenomenal, and the percentages proved it to be highly successful. Robert Raikes did receive the title of "Father of the Sunday School," but one can rightfully designate Methodism, the church denomination that John Wesley started, as one of the major factors in his success. However, success in itself can cause a lot of enemies to surface, and the Raikes movement was no exception to opposition.

The Raikes' Sunday School Movement's success had its opposition. England wanted the masses to be kept in their place during the French Revolution, which was causing the leaders of France to be killed by the guillotine. The conditions in England had dramatically changed as infidelity seemed to prevail and the children and youth personified ignorance and poverty. The church had also become separate from the state, and sectarianism was on the rise.

The clergy seemed to abandon the call to fulfill their duties to provide catechetical ministry. Some of the religious preachers thought it was beneath their dignity to provide instruction to the children of the lower classes. They complained of the children being dirty, and others had the belief that no work of any kind should be done on the Sabbath, stating that it was a sin to use the mind or body on the Holy Day.

Raikes responded by quoting the words of Jesus: "The Sabbath was made for man and not man for the Sabbath." He was also wise enough to implement a compromise by excluding the educational subjects of writing and mathematics from being taught on Sunday.

One positive source of advertisement in addition to Raikes' own newspaper was the *Gentleman's Magazine.* The owners of this magazine printed an article that encouraged an onslaught against the Sunday School Movement. In 1797, the article stated that the Sunday School Movement was a subversive movement away from the peace and tranquility that caused happiness to society and that it was undeserving of encouragement and applause. This was a blow to the movement, but in 1784 the same magazine printed articles that helped the growth spurt in the Ragged School. Some considered the movement worthy of contempt and that the leader of the movement should be exploded rather than being applauded due to his vain vision of the movement. A particular Scottish preacher's objection feared that the Sunday school would destroy the family religion. Raikes saw that he was paving a road with the Ragged School that many did not want to follow and had their own personal misgivings regarding it.

Others such as Charles Wesley and William Wilberforce caught the vision of the movement. Wesley introduced singing in the Sabbath Schools. Wilbert Wilberforce, a member of the English Parliament, was a strong proponent of the Sunday school, and he influenced numerous men of importance to support it. William Wilberforce contributed generously to the Sunday school and provided finances for the printing of Bibles for the children. He was also able to persuade the Queen of England at the time, Queen Charlotte, who was so impressed it brought Raikes a prestigious invitation to the court of England. Raikes stood in the presence of King George and Queen Charlotte and declared that the Ragged School produced such loyal subjects because it formed character and morality among the students and was instrumental in eliminating illiteracy.

The Raikes Ragged School was also instrumental in advancing two of the most major social trends of that time. One was its undeniable influence by providing general education for the poor, and secondly and most important was the decline of child labor. Raikes had the vision that every child, no matter how poor, should attend school. This helped to champion the end of child labor because in order for the children to attend school, they needed ample time free from work. This eliminated the "smug dictum" that educating the masses was perilous. Robert was convinced and had proven from his earlier involvement with the men in prison that ignorance reproduced criminal influences and that morality was inductive to productive living.

His audience with the King and Queen of England provided the platform for the argument that the strength of the country would depend upon the country's ability to educate the children and young people, who in actuality were the future of England. The manufacturers and labor shops resisted any attempt to reduce the children's working hours with stern stubbornness, but Raikes scheduled classes for evening and night and hired and paid for the teachers to teach the kids reading and writing and ciphering.

The imprint that Robert Raikes left on the world with his Sunday school plan explains why he earned the title of "The Father of the Sunday School" because he was a prophet with a vision for the children and the youth. Robert Raikes himself was mistakenly a good man, but it was not until he was reading one of his own students the Scripture in Isaiah, the fifty-third chapter that he received pardon for sin and Christ as Savior.

After retiring from business in the year of 1802, he received an award entitled "the freedom of the city." Robert Raikes passed away in the year 1811 at the age of seventy-six from an illness that lasted for only about thirty minutes. During his funeral, the children from the school he had formed followed his body all the way to the grave, singing Sunday school hymns all the way. He lived long enough to see his dream become fulfilled, which was the shortening of the labor hours for children to attend school. His untiring work was responsible for the formation of the Education Act of 1870 that mandated local authorities to provide schools during the day for all of the children in the British Isles. He had seen what began with twelve boys grow to an army of over a quarter of a million souls in London alone and countless more in Wales, Scotland, Ireland, and even in America. The tiny experiment that began with the impression to "try" was the humble beginning that catapulted Sunday school into the nineteenth century as a very powerful, vivacious tool for moral and religious advancement. This potent formula continued over to the twentieth century and developed the vision beyond measure.

William Foxes' Sunday School

William Fox was a protégé of Robert Raikes, which is the hallmark of any movement. Another philanthropist, a recipient of the potent seed that proved to be a germ of the Sunday school, William Fox was born the same year and same day of the month as Robert Raikes, only not in the same county. These two philanthropists did manage to unite in destinies, and both men were gifted with the sovereign plan for successful youth ministry.

William Fox was born February 14, 1736 in Clapton, England, which was only a few miles northeast of Gloucester, England, where Raikes was born. William was born to Christian parents who were agriculturists. His family was members of the Baptist church in the same town of Clapton. William was the youngest of eight children. His mother was left widowed when William's father died when William was only three years of age. Mrs. Fox was left with a large family, but she did not shrink in light of this grave responsibility to rear her eight children. She was highly intellectual and esteemed as a person of great wisdom and advice.

William was very diligent in his studies, determined to become a profitable businessman to buy the family farm one day. He went to work at a very young age, but the work was too laborious for him and he soon returned home to work on the family farm until he turned seventeen years of age. Eventually, William Fox became an ardent businessman with superb skills and above average business savvy.

His business acts gave a strong witness to his profession of Christianity, and he refused to transact business on the Sabbath day.

Mr. Fox earned an impeccable reputation for his business dealings and soon became a very prosperous individual. He married and moved to London, where he joined the Baptist denomination that he was accustomed to attending. His success at business put him in a position to commence benevolent efforts in favor of education in his native hometown. His first step was to provide clothing for all the poor people in the village—the men, women, and children. The next step he took was to set up a school during the weekdays for the free instruction of all those who were willing to take advantage of the benefits.

The reading in the school was confined to the Bible. Since there was not a chapel in the village, he directed all those in attendance at the school to attend services at the Episcopal church. Mr. Fox's goal all along was that every poor person would be able to read the Bible. This goal proved to be a momentous undertaking because it seemed that he could not find anyone to take the leadership of his project, but Mr. Fox did not give up; he became the leader.

He attended the monthly Baptist meeting and introduced the subject to the leaders so as to secure the adoption of a plan to provide scriptural education to all the poor children by use of the Bible. It was through this meeting that Mr. Fox garnered support and announced his further plans to form—to his knowledge—the first Sunday school society (which was not called a Sunday school society at the time, but was altogether in principal). (Although there were Sunday schools in existence elsewhere, to his knowledge this one was the first). William Fox's vision for the poor children was aimed at reducing poverty and illiteracy, as well as improving the society as a whole by eradicating the apparent ignorance that was rampant among those so young.

William Fox learned of the Robert Raikes Sunday schools and his advertisement of it in the *Gloucester Journal* and saw the similarities of both schools and the same desired result both men desired to obtain. William Fox opened a correspondence with Mr. Raikes on the idea of a universal plan to promote education among the poor. He noted in the letter his previous ignorance of the Raikes Sunday School but requested permission to follow Raikes' successful example in Gloucester.

William Fox has been accredited with the establishment of the first Sunday society in the city of London in September, 1785. The name actually given was "The Society for Promoting Sunday Schools Throughout the British Dominions."

Both Robert Raikes and William Fox were exemplarily men with hearts of genuine philanthropy who unselfishly put aside their denominational differences and united their efforts, further igniting the germ of the Sabbath Schools to the Glory of God and for the good of all mankind. Both men agreed that the Sabbath Schools were the only or most effective means of enabling the unlearned to know what the Scriptures meant and contained, causing a great transformation in the morals and manners of those children and youth who partook of the opportunities that were afforded them at the Sunday schools. Some considered the Sunday school the most effective way to combat juvenile delinquency and crime.

The Formation of the Sunday School Society

The Sunday School Society for the poorer classes experienced more longevity in England than in America. Sunday Schools continued to grow throughout the entire world and were a primary force in developing and shaping the character and morality of the youth. Many denominations adopted the plan, resulting in over sixty million children, youth, and adults receiving the Gospel. America alone comprised of over twenty-five million students in the Sunday School Society by the end of the 19th Century. By the year 1870, Britain and America both established state education as a mandatory provision. Therefore, the public school system was established, which provided for secular education during the weekdays. The Sunday school globally remained a major force for spiritual and biblical literacy for the development of children, youths, and families' knowledge of the Scriptures. However, a downward trend began as parents became permissive in the 1960's, and the culture of insisting that children attend Sunday school, whether or not their parents went, was abandoned.

Chapter IV

THE SUNDAY SCHOOL EMERGENCE IN AMERICA

Early American Sunday Schools can be accounted for as soon as the year 1630, shortly after the early settlers arrived in New England. These settlers had been exposed to the Great Reformation movement and were full of inspiration to share their faith. Arrival to the New World had its own share of hardships, but the settlers, who were also called Pilgrims, did not neglect to provide religious education to their children.

In Massachusetts Bay, the colonists established Harvard College in the year of 1636. The earliest mandated provision for the establishment of religious instruction was ordered in 1642, from the General Court of Massachusetts. The law stated that all masters of families should perform catechism with their children and servants in the principles of religion at least once a week. They were also required to test them to determine what they had learned from the instruction. This religious culture was infiltrated by masters of the families, but the catechizing of youth was the job of the clergymen, who were part of a much larger group that had migrated from England and called themselves Puritans. Methods of catechizing the youth varied among each parish. However, they were effective in getting many youth to complete their studies. Many of them instructed the children on the Sabbath and in the church. Other Puritans that were stricter would gather once a week, or once a month on Saturdays, to teach the children. The Puritan family teaching system was very effective toward training the children spiritually.

Charles Wesley sailed on a missionary journey to America, initially visiting Savannah, Georgia, to establish the Sabbath Schools on the new land in the year 1735. His brother, Charles, accompanied him on the trip. In addition, there were over eighty English colonists and twenty-six Moravian Christians on the voyage as well. John's trip to Savannah was a response to a request by a James Oglethorpe, who had led a group of settlers to Savannah in the year of 1733.

James' intent seemed to be to establish it as a non-slavery colony. He had asked John to serve there as a missionary to both the English who had settled there and to the native tribes in the area. John's trip brought him personal spiritual revelation and spiritual understanding as he observed the devotion and obvious joy that the Moravians exemplified as they sang and worshipped in psalms during the voyage. John noticed certain serenity among the Moravians as the ship experienced sea storms. The Moravians were fearless in the face of the great danger they experienced on the voyage, and they responded to it with joyful singing while all others on the ship, including Wesley, were terrified. This caused Wesley to inwardly question his own religion. They also had a pastor on board the ship named Spangenberg who presented Wesley with questions about his salvation. However, when presented with the question of his own personal assurance of salvation, he could not answer.

He wondered what Christian faith was he proclaiming if he was not sure of his own personal relationship with Jesus Christ. He was an Anglican minister on a missionary journey to America. He was educated and trained for the ministry and deeply religious. He was traveling across an ocean to spread the Christian faith, which he had led others to follow methodically in England, yet he knew that he was missing an element in his own personal relationship with Christ. He had preached powerful messages regarding spiritual discipline, condemned vanity and fancy clothing, and inspired others to new levels of righteousness. He had encouraged sanctified lifestyles and the methodical study of the Scriptures, which was the reason they were called Methodists, but John realized on this voyage that the Moravian Christians had something that he did not have.

In the process of time, John preached in the new colony in Savannah, Georgia. Many of the people responded out of curiosity. It seemed that they were not really sure of what religion John was affiliated with. John started holding small Bible studies on Sunday afternoons. However, he did not really consider his ministry in America to be successful but found it to be very difficult.

It was here that he fell in love with a woman by the name of Sophia Hopkey, whom he pursued in courtship. For some reason, John feared that if he married Sophia, it would be detrimental to his ministry, so he decided against the marriage. The woman soon married someone else, and John Wesley attacked her reputation publicly and openly. This caused John a great deal of stress and harm, as her new husband took Wesley to court for defamation of his new wife's character. After receiving many complaints against him, his popularity waned and he returned to England only after spending two years in America. John considered his missionary journey an utter failure, only to find out later that it was quite the contrary.

Whitfield's Methodist Connection

During John Wesley's Missionary journey to Savannah, he established Christ Church, which was the first Anglican Church of Savannah. What appeared to be a failure in his own eyes was not a failure in the eyes of God. It proved to be a watered and planted seed of the Sabbath Schools that contributed to the Great Awakening of America. While John traveled back to England, George Whitfield, who was a personal friend of Wesley and a member of the Methodist Society that John had established in England, traveled to America from England. Their journeys crossed each other's paths. George Whitfield was a major player in the Great Awakening that was about to take place.

The trip to Georgia would be George Whitfield's first trip to the new colony. While it appeared that John's trip was a failure, George was actually traveling to America to oversee an orphanage in John's parish that he had established during his two-year missionary stay in Savannah. George Whitfield's ministry seemed to pick up where John's had left off.

George had also been a member of the Methodist society in England, and he believed in the righteousness that John preached, but he also had another element because he preached the message of spiritual rebirth. George preached to the people in Savannah, proclaiming that the people must be born again, and his message was eagerly received. Revelation help had come to Georgia from God, by way of Whitfield, to empower the people to live the dedicated, sanctified, and disciplined lives that Wesley had taught them.

Whitfield verified the good that John Wesley had done while in America, realizing that he had laid the foundation for the movement in America. Whitfield proclaimed John as the schoolmaster, the forerunner that God had used to lead the people to hear the message through Whitfield. Whitfield also alluded to his inability to express the good that John Wesley had done in Savannah.

Whitfield's missionary trip to America appeared again to both be the sprout of the seed for the Sabbath Schools and a wakeup call for America. Whitfield's travels led him to Maine, Massachusetts, Delaware, and then back to Georgia. This great awakening impacted America to the point that Benjamin Franklin noted that it seemed as if the whole world was growing religious, for if anyone walked through the towns during the evening, the sounds of different families singing hymns was prominent. The Great Evangelical Awakening forever changed American history. The Great Awakening is reported to then have set blaze in England when Whitfield traveled back to his homeland. He preached under a powerful anointing, but it was not totally accepted by the Church of England—primarily churchgoers who were religious, but not born again.

Nevertheless, many people were drawn to the services, and a revival broke out in Bristol, England. Whitfield sensed the need to return to America, so he invited John Wesley to take over the revival that had exploded in Bristol. Equipped with the great talent for organization, John Wesley soon setup Methodist Societies throughout Great Britain, and he utilized the small group sessions that were successful in his missionary trip to America, which included Bible classes on Sunday afternoon.

This Revival Awakening continued to burn across the American continent, with John Wesley being very instrumental. He began to ordain elders to lead the American Methodist churches. The American Methodist church exploded with the new, trained leadership to guide them, like the way it did in England and Scotland.

America won its independence in 1784, and the open-air services and circuit-riding preachers fit the lifestyle of the American frontiers. As Wesley had organized the children and youth ministries in England, after the society was officially established in America, he communicated that every society should have a book entitled *Instructions for Children.* It included within it the commission to preachers to form children's classes, which led to the organization of the Sunday school.

Initially, in the beginning of the Sunday school movement, all efforts were focused on the Sunday school as a ministry of benevolence. Wesley considered it a mere redirecting and expansion of the religious instruction that obligated the pastor and made him officially responsible for the religious instruction in his church. This is how the early Sunday school was connected to the local church. It rapidly became a church institution, but in Methodism, the Sunday school, which allowed the blessing that was once provided only to the rich to be provided for the poor children as well, replaced the original children's catechetical classes.

Some issues did arise with this new delegation and the transference of the responsibility of leadership to that of the local pastor in the Methodist church. The reason for this is that many of the schools were begun, run, and organized by those with a desire to do so and not the leadership of the church.

William Elliott: Continuous Sunday Schools

A layman began one of the first continuous Sunday schools in America by the name of William Elliott, who had emigrated from England to Virginia in the year 1724. He eventually converted to Methodism around 1772. He started a Sunday school that was held on the Sabbath afternoon in his home in 1785. He instructed white boys and girls, including his own children.

As the word traveled in the neighborhood, friends were admitted. He also extended it to the negro slaves at a different hour. He used the Bible as a textbook and taught everyone how to read the Bible for themselves. The class instruction proved successful, and the Sunday school class was transferred to his church. He became the first superintendent of the Sunday school at the Burkton-Oak Grove Church in Virginia that had begun in 1785 and continued to the celebration of 132 years of aggressive Sunday school effort in a single community.

Policy Changes

The policy change allotted the same lessons to all of the classes and established that the number of Scriptures memorized did not constitute evidence of advancement in divine knowledge and understanding. The aim was to eradicate parrot memorizing and to allow application of the Scriptures due to understanding them and not just memorization. This marked the emergence of what was considered the greatest system of biblical study up until that time.

An essay that won great reward was entitled "The Best Book Of Practical Instruction For Sunday–School Teachers." It suggested the division of the classes according to age and literacy by grouping the younger children from two years to seven years old together. Those not able to read and considered ignorant were grouped into another division, and those from ages seven to fifteen who could read were grouped as “those instructed.” The adult division was established and divided to include anyone over the age of fifteen. It suggested that each division be taught separately in different classrooms for efficiency.

From the very beginning as a result of the initial Missionary journey of John Wesley to America, there was a very close connection between Methodism in America and in England during the years of the Sunday schools’ rapid spread.

Bishop Asbury received a lot of direction from Wesley, and so the educational vision of John Wesley became intertwined with those of American Methodism. The establishment of schools for boys and girls in order to bring Christian education to all, regardless of the size of the town or village, was thoroughly documented in a letter addressed to the Methodist Episcopal Church in America. The letter communicated that the schools should be open two hours for both the morning and evening sessions on the Sabbath.

Asbury seemed to have a vision early on of district schools, suggesting that a president preside over each district or region. This contributed to more growth of the Sunday schools in several different places, but the teachers were still not paid for any services rendered. Asbury students were mostly black children whose parents did not seem committed to sending the children, and Asbury’s teachers were very discouraged. With no pay, they soon gave up the Sunday Schools in these areas.

By the year 1810, Sunday school teachers in America were being paid salaries, which initially began twenty years earlier with implementation of the Robert Raikes Sunday School revival. The contributions to the American Sunday-School Union totaled nearly a million dollars annually, compared to the international charitable contributions, which totaled over twenty-six million annually.[14] Paid teaching of Sunday school teachers soon disappeared as a whole around the middle of the 18th century.

The history of the Sunday school movement in America was greatly assisted by the Methodist Publishing houses, the Book Concern and their depository for religious books and tracts. The Book Concern Christian publishing was begun by a Reverend John Dickens, who began preaching in 1777 and made his first entry to the Book Concern printing in 1789. The first publishing was a small hymn book that he published with his own private funds. The Book Concern publishing was managed with great integrity and had acquiescence of a great degree of magnitude. It was responsible for excellent Scripture-Catechism books, which have been used in the Methodist church for a great length of time because they were so useful. The Book Concern also issued volumes for the libraries of Sunday schools. A popular edition was called *The First Question of Methodism.*

The General Conference of 1824 requested that The Book Concern compile a catechism for the use of Sunday schools and requested that a sufficient inventory of the catechism and a variety of other books for the Sunday schools be kept on hand for immediate use. Initially, the Methodist Church did not have a church depository and literature except for that from The Book Concern.

The Sunday school movement had spread to Philadelphia by the year 1814. This was the first record of a Sunday school in Philadelphia, beginning with thirty-six students and six teachers. They met in a

---

[14] *The History of the Sunday School Movement in the Methodist Episcopal Church.* By Addie Grace Wardie. The Methodist Book concern. New York, Cincinnati.

rent-free room that they had obtained next door to a church. It seems they experienced some rejection from the church and subsequently taught in an open-air burial ground behind the church. Oblivious to the persecution, they continued and eventually prevailed, with a building being erected in the back of the church for their use. Growth came out of their continued perseverance. Seven schools were established near their borders, and five of them were connected to the Union Church, with the attendance being around twelve hundred children.

Baltimore, Maryland, established a Sabbath School Society in 1816 named the McKendrean Female Sabbath School Society. Brooklyn, New York, established a Sabbath Union Sunday School in July 1817. By the year 1825, The Massachusetts Sabbath School Union was formed, and it was considered an auxiliary to the American Sunday School Union that had preceded it.

The Massachusetts Sabbath School Society started in Beverly in the year of 1810. Two women, Joanna Prince and Hannah Hill, were the first teachers. Miss Prince taught a day school in her mother's house at first. Both women were instrumental in teaching in the Sabbath school in the school classroom of Ms. Prince. Classroom times were in the morning and after the afternoon service at church. It began with thirty students. Many of the students were eager to learn to read, while others who already knew how to read practiced Scripture lesson recitals from memory.

Prince and Hill continued the school for three years. A larger room was purchased due to the successful growth, and others joined in on the enterprise. Eventually, a general school was established, and all the societies united with it. Some were very envious of the success, and the Orthodox Congregationalists formed separate parish schools.

The Boston Sabbath School was started by a woman who actually resided in Nashua, New Hampshire. She saw the Sabbath School while she was visiting Beverly, Massachusetts. She was so impressed with the idea that she had only heard about by word of mouth that she immediately began the establishment when she returned home to Boston. It began in the year 1812 and continued through the year 1822. It was sanctioned by the pastor but maintained and managed by the woman, who was known by her devotion and commitment to Christianity in the school as well as in her personal lifestyle. She was wholly accredited for the enterprise, and she received donations of books, Bibles, and New Testaments, and hymnals totaling fifty-four volumes. This donation was the inception of the First Sabbath School Library in Boston, Massachusetts.

The Sunday school was a major force, even in America, for Christian instruction of youth. The effects were far reaching, with missionaries being birthed from the Sunday school system. Sincere workers were forming hundreds and even thousands of Sunday schools. The Sunday school movement was highly organized and made many structural and organizational changes to facilitate the ever-changing environments in the world.

The major influence on children and youth from the biblical standpoint stemmed from the institution of the Sabbath by God and the command to perpetuate the teachings. The Sabbath schools were the initial force that birthed the Sabbath Schools, as evidenced in the Bible and in Jewish culture. The plan of God was to influence generations both socially and morally with the ever-powerful eternal Scriptures. The birth of the Sunday school from the germ of the

Sabbath Schools continued to infuse this vision and assignment. However, as times change and people change, new strategies needed to be forged to continue the eternal assignment. The Sabbath Schools and the Sunday Schools played their eternal roles, but new plans and procedures transcended to further the daunting task.

Chapter V

CATHOLIC CHURCH YOUTH STRATEGIES

The Young Christian Workers movement began in the year 1938 and had the unique vision to educate and form "lay apostles" within the Roman Catholic Church. The vision of the YCW was basically to empower laypeople in mid-twentieth-century Catholicism. The YWC movement was in sharp contrast to the traditional hierarchy of the Catholic Church, which included Popes, Cardinals, Archbishops, bishops, and priest.

The origin of the YCW was in Belgium and was eventually imported to the United States. The movement was actually birthed by Canon Joseph Cardijn who made a pledge on his fathers' deathbed to dedicate his own life to improving the quality and training of Christian workers. His father had died before his time due to exertion in Christian work. Cardijn was first assigned as a priest in the year 1912. He began to have meetings with the youth and held small group discussions, and from these meetings, he developed a series of actions that he considered pertinent and became known as the three-step system of Observer, Judge and Act.

The three-step system had considerable impact on the Catholic Church, as the youth were leaving the church in droves, sensing that the church could not relate to them. With the birth of Marxism, they had other negative influences they were gravitating to. Cardijn had the foresight to see that the lay apostles were the decisive factor in the future of the world and the salvation of mankind. He believed that the church would be more impacted for the cause of Christ by training and developing one person at a time, starting with the young people. YCW would be the tool that would ignite the emigrational return of the church to the people and the people to the church. Cardijn believed that each individual had a divine purpose and a divine assignment to be fulfilled and executed in this present life.

The church at Rome officially recognized YCW in the year of 1925, and the growth spurt began throughout all of Europe from there. The movement took flight and proved to be an impressive challenge to the standard Marxist belief that seemed to have captured and opiated the masses. Marxism was becoming increasing popular in Europe, and the YCW was a formidable response to this movement that was challenging Christianity, as it resembled and represented the very essence of Christianity.

The Observer, Judge, and Act movement had a mobilizing effect on small groups and was effective in mobilizing the threefold process entitled the social inquiry. The "Observe" step involved a detail gathering of data that was to be investigated and diagnosed in every individual situation. This step involved sharing specific details within the group what they had seen over the past week on a topic assigned at each prior meeting. The intent of the Observe strategy was to awaken workers through discourse to various practices and to help them communicate about the situations in which they worked and on a daily basis. The topics they discussed included family life, socialism, and capitalism, and included all aspects of the human associations that fell into the category of what was considered Catholic actions.

The second step in the process of the social inquiry procedure was called "Judge." The youth of Catholicism had primarily been taught their faith through catechism and study and had affirmed their teaching through baptism and sacramental rites of passage during confirmation. Rites of passage are considered by some to be a ritual event that charts a person's progress from one stage to another. Various professions such as Anthropologist and Sociologist, consider rite of passage is an uncommon phenomenon and displays the values and beliefs that vary from culture to culture. When we speak of the rites of passage, we are referring to the moral code based on biblical standards that are the foundation for morality.

However, in the modern sense, rites of passage are also considered to be events related to birth, becoming an adult, marriage status, and even death. This also includes initiation ceremonies such as baptism, confirmation, and Bar or Bat Mitzvah, which are rites of passages for Judaism.

Rites of Passage

As it relates to biblical instruction and its impact on those who actually put into practice, other techniques with the same aim can produce very positive results as well such as: Rites of Passage. Rites of passage in its entirety consist of three phases: separation, transition, and reincorporation. Separation, which is the first phase of the rites of passage, is where a withdrawal takes place and the individual makes the preparation to move from one place to another. There are symbolic steps as well as acts of detachment or a "cutting away" from the former self. Ideally, the Bar and Bat Mitzvah occur when Jewish children reach thirteen years of age for boys and twelve years of age for girls. They go through an actual ceremony detailing all the phases of the rites of passage. In Orthodox Jewish culture, the young man is called to read the Torah, usually during Shabbat or one of the Jewish festival services, and is required to give a "d'var Torah," a discussion of that week's Torah portion. In non-Orthodox Jewish congregations, similar services are required for the young ladies transitioning through puberty or at the age of twelve. The separation phase of the rites of passage is clearly demonstrated in the Bar and Bat Mitzvah's, as the young people exit adolescence and are made fully responsible for following Jewish law as adults. Here again another method for teaching and training as demonstrated in these definite truths as taught in Sunday School classes as well.

Other responsibilities include moral responsibility and accountability for their own actions; eligibility to be called to read from the Torah and participate in a Minyan, the possession of personal property; may be legally married; and the requirement to observe the 613 laws of the Torah. The reading from the Torah or being called to say the blessing during a service is called an Aliyah, which means "to rise, to ascend or to go up." The Bar Mitzvah celebration usually precedes a celebration meal with family and friends and others in the Jewish community. The wearing of the tefillin is also a significant part of the separation phase of the rites of passage as a symbolic act of the Bar Mitzvah activities.

Some other examples of rites of passage include the act of cutting the hair when a person has joined the military, which is also a part of the transition phase. The transition (or luminal) phase is the period between states, during which one has left one place or state but has not entered or joined the next. The third phase, reincorporation, is consummated by the performance of the actual ritual itself. Once the ceremony or ritual is completed, the final phase has taken place and the new identity has been established or confirmed.

Rites of passage do vary depending upon the culture, and are not always equal, however they share the commonality in the stages and it may be at different degrees in the three stages. They all comparatively include the following: a period of segregation from everyday life, a luminal state of transition from one status to the next, and a process of reintroduction to the social order with a new standing.

Again, our reference for the purpose of this research is to emphasize those practices that produce morality that is in line with the biblical teachings of Christ. Since the birth of the New Testament church, repentance, the new birth or being born again, water baptism, communion, Holy Spirit baptism, and sanctification are rites of passage according to the Christian faith.

Some other rites of passages symbols include: First Eucharist and first confession (especially First Communion in Catholicism), confirmation (most Christian denominations, such as Catholic, Orthodox, and mainline Protestant churches), confirmation in Reform Judaism, Bar Mitzvah and Bat Mitzvah in Judaism, circumcision (mainly in Judaism), and diving for the cross (in some Orthodox Christian churches). Multiple aspects of teaching responsibility, discipline and morality require innovation, just as long as the desired result is accomplished.

Young Christian Workers

The youth in the YWC had been provided scriptural, moral guidelines in which to gauge their consciences, and the rights of passage engineered a significant part as the definite goal remained the same which was to teach the youth and provide instruction as in the Sunday School that can attribute to behavior the Scripture promotes. These activities were general and were not specifically related to the lives of the workers. In YCW, the youth formed practices of discernment and judgment that were instrumental in challenging them to relate the Gospel and teachings of the church to the situations in their own everyday lives. The guiding questions that they asked their consciences during the process was, "Is this Christian?" (which is similiar to a Twenty-First Century question that youth coined, "What would Jesus do?"). The young workers could compare what they observed during the week to the teachings of the church. The YCW had to identify vices such as greed, misery, and isolation and acts that were considered unjust including other social teachings that presented themselves as a problem.

Cardijn was convinced that the first two steps alone were not enough to adequately assist in the transformation of the youth into lay apostles. The "Act" step involved the youth putting into practice specific practices in response to the behavior or situations they had Observed and Judged. They could be individual or group improvements in moral behavior, attitudes, and collective actions, such as attendance to Mass or organizing a strike.

Cardijn initially wanted the YCW to become like a young labor union, although it was not limited to that. They were awakened to a new view of their world, and it challenged them to judge social problems and to respond as adults in faith. For those young people who were committed to YCW, the Social Inquiry became a way of life as lay apostles.

Theoretically, the YCW was based on the foundations of the sacraments of the church. It was through the sacraments of the Eucharist that the YCW members were committing themselves to live a community life that was a reflection of the Mystical Body of Christ. As married couples, the members committed themselves to live lives of unselfish love and to devote themselves to their children. As they went through the confirmation process, they accepted the responsibilities of being lay apostles. This included being effective Christian witnesses and Christian influences in total dedication to the Christian life. Upon confirmation to the YCW, this was also called the Mystical Body of Christ. They also created cell groups. The YCW movement received affirmation by the Pope in the year of 1926, eventually spread to France, and then expanded to include over forty-eight countries.

The Joist Program, JOC

The YCW, also known by its French acronym of JOC, (Jeunesse Ouvrière Chrétien) spread to America in the city of Brooklyn, New York, from 1938 through 1939. Paul McGuire was an Australian Catholic activist that the Knights of Columbus invited to speak in America. After the Brooklyn laymen heard the inspirational discourse of McGuire, a layman by the name of John Barker received council and approval from the priest in the area and began to meet with small groups of laity there in New York to form their own YCW cell. The American groups met, and discussions were on the normal topics of the traditional JOC, such as working environments, engagement and marriage topics, recreation, and family life in general.

The American YCW members called themselves American Jocists, and at their meetings, the members were expected to bring in information on each topic of discussion. Some of the early campaigns for the American Joists were for decent movies, restoring lethargic Catholics by encouraging them to return to sacraments, working with the department stores to create more Christmas type displays in celebration of the Christmas holidays, and the use of religious cards for display purposes.

The American Joists had their share of opposition and difficulties. Some of the cells were not able to fully grasp the theological translation of what the JCW called the Mystical Body of Christ. Since the priest guided the laity of the Catholic Church for so many years, most of them did not have access to the Scriptures, the YCW members' struggled with the interpretation of the faith and its application. During its early years, the meetings were not combined to include males and females. The Young Christian Workers felt that they should be able to accurately give an answer if they were going to contend for the faith and grow in knowledge of the faith they preached.

Another barrier they faced was the isolation of the members due to the YCW leaders not agreeing to affiliate with the other Catholic youth programs that were founded by the Catholic Church. The premise was that the YCW was radically different from the other programs, and they isolated themselves from because the various youth programs were focused more on the religious and personal behavior of the laity, but the YCW was more focused on problems of social justice.

The reluctance to merge with other youth groups within the Catholic Church could produce failure for any movement. The bishop and priest were a huge part of the success or failure because starting the local YCW programs and other programs required endorsement by the leaders of the church. Another hindrance to the JOC program was the immoral lifestyles of some of the YCW members. Some of the members were seen exemplifying behavior that was indifferent to the cause itself, and this was detrimental to the cause, vision, and reputation of the YCW, which was to become the Mystical Body of Christ and to form lay apostles. This riotous behavior became a target for those looking for reasons to point the finger at Catholicism and Christianity. Accommodations were made by those considered the upper class of the Church due to the infiltration of communism in America.

The YCW used every tool at their disposal to distance the movement from communism and continue the assignment from its origin to form lay apostles of Christ who practiced the steps of Observer, Judge, and Act as YCW. The YCW still had the perception as Young Christian Workers, but the focus shifted to a general youth movement and not a youth workers movement. The movement was considered a grass roots movement that had a spiritual formation but transitioned again in its position to a top-down directed movement and began to be referred to as a middle class educational movement. The leaders of the American YCW had to make the adjustment to differentiate them as a practice and scripturally based movement.

Inevitably, the American YCW adopted the European model and made it more intrinsic with American culture. The reason for this was to acclimate it to the American working class and to persuade them to return to the church and to act out their faith. Although adapted from Europe's model, the American model persisted in appealing to the benefits of the individual rather than the masses.

The small group members felt a sense of belonging that is not usually felt when memberships in large organizations are acquired.

In its infancy, the YCW stressed practices that were instrumental in obtaining conversions instead of allowing the conversions to take place first, giving the converts the tools to put into practice what they had learned. The unfortunate part of this accommodation for the YCW was that conversions to Christianity took a back seat to practicing service, as was stated in the three-step process of Observe, Judge, and Act. The American YCW continued to modify its program and instituted combined cell meetings of male and female cell groups. As the YCW observed the successful collaboration of the combined female and male groups, they were intent on continuing the idea, and it initiated the standard of mixed groups across the United States.

During this time, the knowledgeable women learned to act ignorant to allow for the less trained men to have a perception of control, allowing them to feel like they were in charge. Some of the males were not accustomed to the young women voicing their opinions in the meetings and had to make adjustments. Along with the opportunity for the young males, the YCW enabled the young lay-women to communicate their faiths in ways that were non-traditional to the church. The YCW considered that service was the life of the YCW, and their services included improving working conditions and various other labor-related activities. One of their goals was that they championed economic reform as it related to women.

The early formation of the YCW Joist program was in how it accommodated the Catholic youth, but encouraged the youth to resist the American culture. Racism was still a major issue in America during the 19th century. The YCW members worked to ensure that the restaurants in a certain city provide equal service to blacks. They performed a survey to see which restaurants were actually complying with the law that prohibited discrimination to blacks. They aimed to personally Christianize and educate the fine American city. Tensions arose in America, but the YCW was able to formulate the abilities to adapt as well as resist through patriotism.

The YCW participants had to adapt to the changing facets of the new era of music. Rock and roll had become increasing popular, and the YCW youth, like other youth of their time, had to adapt to the changing face of music, yet keep their Christianity. The Mystical Body of Christ doctrine did not align itself with the rock and roll movement of the time. By 1957, over one-third of the youth involved in the YCW were considered white-collar employees, with only a small fraction of them being blue-collar workers. The leaders of this era of the YCW attempted to keep the movement's focus by concentrating on domestic issues such as joblessness, worker safety, and sexual harassment, but the difficulty surfaced because the distinction of the movement's identity as a Catholic workers movement and an American Youth movement was not visible. The growth of the movement was stunted because of the confusion associated with its identity, resulting in a name change in 1964 from Youth Christian Workers to YCM or Young Christian Movement.

The YCW continued with its early mission to train and form young workers in a concentrated path as lay apostles. They offered some one-month leadership training courses for those leaders that were willing to take advantage of it. The training offered sessions that educated the leaders more on the apostolic spirit of the movement, the movement's techniques, organizational skills, leadership skills, and instructions on how to follow the YCW meeting model as well as how to actively draw others into participating in Mass. The training was intense, covering training as well on labor and issues of international significance.

The training provided the opportunity for the young leaders to follow the initial practices and the vision steps of Observe, Judge, and Act. The training inspired several acronyms with the intent to further clarify the description of the movement and to somehow avoid further controversy regarding its vision, into national prominence and direction as a youth program titles such as the YCM, namely the YCW, JOC and Joist. The training courses were national and were very effective at communicating the continued purpose and aim of the movement.

The training initiative produced many strong leaders that complimented the YCW movement for a brief time. One leader by the name of Zotti began as a lay apostle in a parish in the city of Chicago, yet in two years' time, she became a national representative at the international meeting in Europe, where the YCW movement was originally birthed. She published her own personal history of the movement that had been instrumental in her development in a publication named *A Time of Awakening.*

The training was considered to be very intense yet refreshing and was considered the pinnacle of formation. As successful as the training was, it did not eliminate criticism by some who considered it to be an educational movement.

The YCW clamored to provide a sense of practicality and relevance for the everyday life experiences of its members and to help them to share with those they intended to recruit. As the movement continued to struggle and to reclaim its identity, they focused on a series entitled The Seven Areas of Life. These seven areas refocused on work and the economics of life, parenting and married life, citizenship and political life, as well as global relations, relations of race, and the life that was traditional to Catholicism, namely the parish life. Some still viewed the YCW as a movement that focused on education, and the argument was that the Youth did not just want education, they wanted a program that addressed their personal needs that they faced everyday individually. The entire goal of the YCW was to empower the lay people of the church, especially the youth, and it succeeded in doing so at a relatively high level. The demise of the movement did not occur cataclysmically but happened gradually with no great alarms.

Youth Christian Movement, YCM

During the 1960s, the YCW partnered with various agencies such as the AFL-CIO, the National Committee on Agricultural Labor, the President's Committee on Children and Youth, and the NAACP. The CORE meetings continued until 1978, but the cells had already begun a slow process of decline. The program that comprised the seven areas, as well as social changes and the Vatican II, seemed to render the emphasis of the YCM program ineffective.

The Vatican II was the Second Sacred Ecumenical Council of the Vatican held by the Catholic Church. This council meeting opened in 1962 under Pope John XXIII after two years of preparation to address several issues that the bishops were facing due to changes in political, social, economic, and technological arenas. The Catholic Church continued the training of lay apostles, but new methods were implemented. Some of these were the Catholic or Parochial schools. Programs such as Confraternity of Christian Doctrine, CYO, World Youth Day, and Jesuit Volunteer Corps provided the emphasis that was more welcomed as times changed for YCW. The Catholic "theology of God's people" replaced the Mystical Body of Christ as the heart cry for the Catholics to become equally as involved in the social arena as they were in the YCW.

The history of the YCW in the United States spanned about thirty years. During this time, the American Catholic Church modified the

European version of the Jocists' program to fit the culture in America. It was a very effective transformational process that was responsible for the reformation of young Catholics by inspiring them to apply their faith to their personal and national lives, instead of allowing it to mold. Many youth became thoroughly grounded in the theology of Catholicism and were instrumental in changing society for the better by becoming active citizens instead of being dormant citizens in society.

The imprint that the YCW left on the youth was indelible, and because they seemed to grasp a better understanding, they were more prepared for the changes that took place when the Vatican II instituted changes at the demise of the YCW. Many of the young Catholic assimilated into the mainstream of society with complete confidence. The contribution that the YCW played in the lives of American Catholics and culture cannot be taken lightly.

Chapter VI

BILLY GRAHAM AND YOUTH FOR CHRIST MINISTRY STRATEGIES

Another superficial outgrowth in youth ministry was the phenomena of the international Youth for Christ that evolved out of the revivalist tradition in American religious history. During the early 1800s, the Great Awakening took place in America, spearheaded by Charles Finney, a lawyer who converted to a preacher. Many Christians were revived, converted, and motivated, causing a rise in patriotism and purity, as well as social reform.

Evangelist Dwight L. Moody and Billy Sunday contributed to the Great Awakening revivals that were considered a part of the third wave of revivals that swept the United States between the years of 1890 through 1920. A major division was created sometime after the year 1920 amid radical changes in the American culture, along with Protestantism. One was the Modernists, who seemed to accommodate ideas such as science, criticism, and pluralism, and the second was the fundamentalists who were very biblical and to some degree were considered conservative extremes such as Holiness, Pentecostal and Fundamental camps that were viewed by some as hostile.

Included in the latter were the Evangelicals, who believed in the imminent return of Christ. The Evangelicals continued to build colleges, churches, campgrounds, and Christian academies, while they expectantly waited on the various pluralism movements and modernist movements such as rapture of the church to occur. American morality had reached new lows, and the Evangelicals needed a way to garner the public attention as a way to confront the decline. There were three of these Evangelical non-denominational youth movements that developed after World War II, and Youth for Christ, better known as YFC, was one of them that ignited the American scene.

Youth for Christ began on the east coast as a ministry to young military men and women in 1940 and immediately after World War II. This idea spread mostly to the east coast locations such as New York City and Washington D.C., as well as Detroit Michigan, Indianapolis Indiana, and St. Louis Missouri. Youth for Christ was officially organized and recognized in the year of 1944 in Winona Lake, Indiana, by four Evangelicals. They received financial support from a Chicago businessman by the name of Herbert J. Taylor. In the year 1945, the organizers, Lloyd Bryant, Percy Crawford, Jack Wyrtzen, and Torrey Johnson chose Billy Graham to be the YFC's first full-time traveling Evangelist.

Youth Rally Explosion in Chicago

After some success, the Youth for Christ movement exploded in the Midwest when Torrey Johnson, who was the pastor of Midwest

Bible Church in Chicago scheduled some youth rallies at the Chicago Orchestra Hall on Saturday nights for a period of twenty-one consecutive weeks. He coordinated half hour radio spots to occur at the same time as the youth rallies were in session. The first rally was preached by Billy Graham, and at the conclusion of the twenty-one weeks, a victory rally was held to support the American alliances in the war. This victory rally drew over twenty-eight thousand young people to Chicago's Soldier Field Stadium.

One year after the victory rally, a Youth for Christ rally was held and the crowd had literally almost doubled to fifty thousand young people. After this magnitude of successful revivals, Chicago became the organizational center for YFC. The blueprint for the rallies with the radio broadcast coordinated with the rallies became the calling card for the YFC. News spread of the rallies, and the attention of the public had been gained. Billy Graham was true to the Evangelical message, as his preaching focused on conversion for Christ.

He urged those in attendance at the rallies to give their heart to Christ and confirm their decision by raising their hands or standing. The converts were given a copy of the Gospel of John to read and were directed to join a local church that believed and taught the Bible in truth. The converts were then encouraged to continue to attend the YFC meetings and to share their newfound faith by becoming immediate witnesses for Christ.

In addition to conversions for Christ, the rallies showed considerable support for the war. World War II was presented as a positive service for Christ and to the United States, and special recognition was given toward the military service men and women in attendance for honorable mention, as they combined the Gospel with patriotism. Some were not enthused about the parallel that was used to depict the war as a holy crusade, since the original Crusades were not a positive historical witness to Christianity.

The selection of Billy Graham as the leader of the YFC movement proved to be a monumental decision that engineered growth in the movement. Graham was converted to Christ as a youth himself, and he became the exemplary role model of the witness of the YFC. Graham represented the embodiment of American virtue and was admirable and clean cut. His every sermon called upon the youth to convert, providing only two choices: either accept Christ and believe Him or die without Him and suffer judgment at the Great White Throne of Judgment.

The YFC rallies continued and reached their pinnacle in the year of 1957. The rallies followed the same format of Saturday night in a big auditorium, lively gospel music, athletes giving their personal testimonies, the special recognition for military and civic leaders, and a short powerful sermon that climaxed with the invitation for those in the audience to come forward and receive Christ.

The YFC meetings featured innocence, heroism, and loyalty to the American dream. Many soldiers testified to the new birth that they experienced at the YFC rallies. The pattern of life that YFC encouraged among the converts was essential in the establishment of their resolute decisions. YFC encouraged a number of habits for the youth to make a part of their daily lifestyles.

The first habit was to read the Scriptures daily. YFC members favorably followed the habit of reading their Bibles. One YFC international vice president for India preferred morning study of the Bible before breakfast. He even stated that he liked reading it through several times a year and he made comments of his study. One YFC person wrote that he expected to meet God Himself when he read the

Bible. The quantity of these instructions was priceless and communicated the infallibility of the Bible. This infallibility was the foundation of the beliefs that the YFC supported.

The Evangelicals

The National Association of Evangelicals was established in the same year as the YFC, and their core beliefs were very much in sync. The statement of faith was included in every publication that the YFC printed, beginning in 1946. *The Youth for Christ Magazine* intentionally reminded the YFC members of the infallibility of the Bible, the Trinity, the Deity of Christ, the miracles of Jesus, and salvation through regeneration by the person of the Holy Spirit. The magazine stressed the commandment to live a holy life and all of the fundamental doctrines of Christ were reiterated. The policy of the YFC meetings was purely non-political, sought exclusion from sectarian and non-political, and would not conflict with the worship services of the local churches. It also encouraged support of world missions.

YFC was insistent about Bible study and beliefs, but they encouraged the young Christians to maintain and become members of various Evangelical organizations. Some of these movements were Legion, Miracle Book Clubs, and High School Born Againers, Singspiration, New Life Boys Ranch, and Word of Life fellowship, which had sprung up close to the same time that YFC had emerged.

Young Life was an Evangelical organization that was founded by another evangelist by the name of Jim Rayburn in 1941. Young Life had a Bible club of youth that actually met in their homes and in the schools, and they used contemporary methods to minister to the youth such as skits, karaoke, and singing.

By 1955, YFC saw the need to become more innovative, and they started the YFC Bible club meetings globally. Many of the clubs met in the high schools, with the intent of reinforcing the teachings during weekdays, where the application of a teaching is lived out in everyday opportunities and not just on Sundays or at church settings. YFC made the youth realize that the high schools were actually pagan and that each YFC member had an assignment to be a witness for Christ in their schools, where YFC believed that missionaries were made.

It was very easy to participate in YFC after high school, since Evangelical Bible colleges had blossomed in the middle of the century. Many of the youth were encouraged to join the clubs such as the Intervarsity Christian Fellowship or Campus Crusade for Christ, which were very comparable to the high school ministries of YFC and Young Life. These were a healthy alternative to secular or modernist schools and were training grounds for activists who had the possibility of impacting the American political climate. What began as a revival of purity shifted to a movement of empowerment to practice what was planted in the seeds of the youth.

YFC advocated individual piety and purity, but they also were instrumental in teaching the youth how to pray effectively. Billy Graham crusades, even apart from the YFC rallies, were highly successful, as he confirmed due to the prayer behind the scenes. The youth reported regularly on the effects that the prayers had in their everyday lives. According to YFC, prayer was both a necessary requirement in order to be effective witnesses for Christ. To the Evangelical, prayer is the key that causes it all to come together stay together. The YFC movement remained consistent as far as membership goes from the 1060s up until around the year 2000. YFC was very aggressive at developing new strategies and assisting in their creation.

The new developments fell under five basic categories. There were the clubs, camps, new-style rallies or spectacle ministries, professional leadership training, as well as educational ministries and social-service ministries. Germs that stemmed as a result of the Youth for Christ movement focused primarily on individual conversion and one-on-one witnessing. YFC was still a very large movement that focused on confirmations, but they did shift from the vision of purity to include practices, which was basically to help youth to apply what they were learning in everyday use. The YFC movement dug deeper and pioneered new creative ministries that included a range of programs to assist with being New Testament Christians in an ever-changing environment.

By 1960, the grassroots movement of Youth for Christ was the YFC Bible clubs, which were later named Campus Life. Campus Life reported over two hundred local offices across the United States alone, with greater numbers internationally. Most of the YFC local chapters were run by a full-time youth minister along with staff and was also sustained by many volunteers. Campus Life ministers weekly through the vehicles of club meetings, home visitations, church meetings, and through the local junior and senior high schools. The format includes an icebreaker, with Bible study, drama skits, and relevant music along, with collaborations on the pressing issues that exist in the lives of youths. The meetings were generally pretty short and last for about an hour. They work hard at getting the youth to become transparent and to open their minds to the Bible. They are also taught how to improve family relations and friendships and are constantly reminded of the love of God. As the meetings progress, the amount of information, as it relates to God, is increasingly poured into the youth.

Campus Life seemed to adopt the vision of a relational ministry that initiated the need for counseling ministries to go along with the Campus Life programs in the United States. YFC was a supporter of the international programs Habitat for Humanity, World Vision, and many social Christian organizations. As new leaders arose, new programs did too and Youth for Christ developed another plan called the Youth Guidance Program. They also realized that they needed to expand their outreach to the urban areas.

The Youth Guidance Program began to operate as many as 110 summer camps for juvenile delinquents by the year of 1963. Like most YFC programs, this one proved to be very successful, and expansions included manuals, lesson plans, and other materials ministry to youth that were in the juvenile system, substance abuse treatment centers for youth, and those youths living in group homes. The summer camp programs remained a vigorous outreach of the YFC but were now expanded to include all youths and not just the middle- and upper-class youth.

Another youth outreach was the Word of Life movement that was started by one of the founding leaders of YFC namely Jack Wyrtzen. These were weeklong meetings that included games, songs, and teaching on relationships, which concluded with a Friday night campfire session. This campfire meeting provided the opportunity for the youth to share their personal testimonies openly and also provided transparency.

Jesus People Ministry

As generations changed, YFC, along with other Evangelical organizations, have adapted the style of the rallies to the various tastes of the adolescents in order to minister to groups like the punk rockers. The Jesus Festival was one such Evangelical outreach that attracted crowds of up to 30,000 youth. Pastor Tony Campolo was a pastor and sociologist who saw something occurring among the punk rock type crowds in the Jesus Festival type meetings.

The Jesus People festival in the United States originated in the early 1970s and was basically a Christian rock music festival. It arose in response to the Woodstock festival, which was totally pagan and opposed all morality that the YFC movement represented. Young people came together to fellowship with others in the body of Christ, but music was a critical component of the fellowship. Tony Campolo was a speaker at these events. He depicted bands rocking to the beat of drums, and giving the personal testimonies of those in the bands who found Christ were attractive to those in the audience, who came forth by the hundreds to receive Christ. Campolo thought it somewhat resembled a marketing strategy for the rock music-hungry contemporary Christian audience, but he felt it did not produce strong disciples of Christ.

Youth Specialties was another separate germ that grew out of the Youth for Christ movement. This ministry was unique in that it offered a variety of capable tools to assist in the leadership and offered training for Evangelical youth ministers. They published a catalog semi-annually that offered teaching tools, videos, discussion starter books, and programming tools for youth ministry. They supplied instructions for forming leaders and all kinds of materials, including lots of books and journals, dramas, and clip art for youth ministries as well.

Youth Specialties published two youth journals named *Youth Workers* and the *Youth Worker Update.* The update version was a monthly newsletter that collected facts from a multitude of sources. The *Youth Worker* was a quarterly update of practical tips and substantive analysis that focused on popular, relevant topics for youth, including sexuality. Some of the articles covered subjects such as "youth worker roundtables," "The sexual youth pastor," "ministry to bisexual teenagers," and "the big m."

This information put the Evangelicals in touch with the most current and prevalent issues among the youth. Just as the YFC movement launched its campaign for the youth, it launched its campaign for international mission with the same vigor and vitality. The Evangelicals were responsible for the development of international missions' programs that involved the youth, which helped them to sense the compassion for others who did not have the liberties, or the opportunities that the American youth had in YFC.

World Vision

Youth for Christ is most famous for its world mission enterprise, World Vision. World Vision promotes community-based mission developments around the entire globe. They provide disaster relief and emergency assistance, and they focus specifically on the needs of children. The Youth for Christ World Vision youth participate annually in what they call a 30 Hour Famine. The local youth groups participate in fasting food for thirty hours to raise funds for World Vision by way of pledges and learning together about world hunger and starvation with the use of educational materials that the agency provides for them. In the year 1998, over 226,000 youth participated in the 30 Hour Famine program and raised over six million dollars for the support of World Vision.

World Vision was only one of multiple agencies that were launched during the sixties that impacted the youth to become more familiar with others that were hurting because of poverty, disease, and natural disasters. Youth for Christ carried the torch and made it a priority to bring morality back to the youth of America. Purity was a major concern, as well as acts of compassion and practical victorious Christian living. If the eternal vision of Youth for Christ faltered, the consequences would have been irreparable for the American culture and the impact on Christianity would have been enormous with the salvation of many compromised.

Chapter VII

YOUTH MINISTRY IN THE AFRICAN AMERICAN CHURCH

One of the most challenging areas of youth ministry can be found within the African American church, and at the same time, it presents one of the most exciting areas of youth ministry. The civil rights movement dramatically changed the role of the Christian in the African American church. To adequately explore this, the history of the African American church after slavery must be considered.

Maya Angelo was a member of the graduating class of 1940 at a training high school in Stamps, Arkansas, at an all-black school in Lafayette County. As a youth, some discriminating remarks made by a politician regarding the goals and aspirations that the class should strive for, which were very limited and included becoming maids and farmers, handymen and washerwomen, were indelibly imprinted on her mind. The next voice she heard was that of the class valedictorian launching his speech to the class entitled "To Be or Not to Be." The valedictorian began to sing the famous negro anthem "Lift Every

Voice And Sing," at the end of his speech. This song rang of freedom of harmony and liberty and is consistent with the efforts and struggles of African American youth in the aftermath of slavery. Angelo recalls a sense of pride with the sudden realization that she had a choice in setting new goals for her educational future.

Bethel A.M.E. Church

The church has been instrumental in the networking of Christian young people in congregations across America. African-American churches have globally instituted and empowered young men and women who helped tremendously with the social practices of the nineteenth and twentieth centuries. Historically, the Bethel African Methodist Episcopal church in Baltimore, Maryland, has been a trailblazer for the African American youth and their development for over two hundred years.

In the year of 1785, several small groups of Christians met in homes and made the decision to form their own congregation after feeling restricted in the churches they attended. This congregation was one of the first, and they named it Beth-el, which in Hebrew means "House of God." This was one of many beginnings for African American youth to rise from oppression to freedom of worship. This church joined with the African Methodist Episcopal denomination and became the center of activity for the abolitionist activities. The church forged ahead socially as it served as a training ground for abolitionist speakers during the time of the Underground Railroad. Bethel led the support in higher education for African Americans. This church alone assisted in sending over seventy-five young African men and women to divinity and seminary schools over a thirteen-year period. Bethel produced these influential leaders, generated social and culture reformations effectively creating a path of success for generations of young people.

It was during the year of the great depressions, that Bethel became the headquarters for the City-Wide Young Peoples forum. The youth director for this agency was Juanita Jackson, who also later became the youth director for the National Association for the Advancement of Colored People. The NAACP was a proud sponsor that aided in the intellectual development and the talents of young African Americans. Bethel's youth in coordination with the National Urban League formed boycotts of the chain stores in the city and picketed the stores for not hiring any negro clerks. They held mass meetings against desegregation and protested the lynchings in 1932-33.

Bethel was instrumental in the diversity of the police department, with the hiring of two black police officers in the city of Baltimore. Bethel church's sanctuary held over sixteen hundred people. They held meetings to discuss the issue of representation on the police force and other crucial social matters in the community. It was through this medium that each Sunday, the young black Christians learned and practiced a form of liberation theology long before they acquired the name of Christian Theology.

Between the years 1930s and the 1950s, Bethel's young people were involved in various traditional styles of youth ministry activities that included Bible study and prayer and of course singing. Bethel's ministry for the youth encompassed music and preaching during their youth services on Sunday mornings.

Segregation was still a stronghold in the United States of America during this time, and by law blacks were still excluded from fully participating in American society. They held some social events that were considered highly significant, which included fashion shows with black models that sent a positive message to young adults enroot from childhood to adolescence that their bodies were indeed beautiful.

Mayme Tilghman was responsible for events that demonstrated economic empowerment for the African Americans of Bethel. She held a fundraiser to collect trading stamps that included a committee to lick the stamps, which raised enough money to buy a school bus for the Sunday school and youth programs. These and other events built self-esteem and insight into the black youths, and they began to learn what freedom meant as it related to liberty from oppression and taking social responsibility for their actions.

The Church has proved to be an institution that has been economically independent in the black community. The Bethel church was a significant figure and played a strategic role in the community in Baltimore as a champion against desegregation. The youth of Bethel recruited other young people to a "March for Baltimore" with four thousand participants led by the activist Dick Gregory. They marched for equal housing and equal access to other benefits of life in modern America.

Many leaders of the civil rights movement met with the Bethel youth to allow them to glean from them. One of the leaders was Thurgood Marshall, who was a native of Baltimore and won fame in the Supreme Court case Brown vs. Board of Education. This famous case paved the way in the fight to alleviate segregation in the United States. Thurgood Marshall was celebrated by the Bethel church for his accomplishments with a grand reception.

Bethel demonstrated through the year 1970 on how to impact young people by teaching them values and using living examples that can teach the values of freedom that are applicable for everyday life.

The Bethel church of Baltimore was a stable force with a proven record that helped to dramatically shape the youth and American society during the time of the civil rights movement.

African American Churches

As with any other movement that is biblically based, the African American church had its own share of critics. Furthermore, not all African American churches were connected to the civil rights movement. Some critics described the African-American religious experience as a type of numbing drug or opiate that pacified blacks in the face of oppression.

Black churches were considered theologically conservative and some critics said they represented the traditional view of theology that was like a tunnel vision that was not concerned with social issues. Critics also said that a compelling number of black congregations wanted to stifle the traditional style of worship that the black churches had become too known by characteristically, especially the African Methodist Episcopal Church. Some of the expressions were the ring-shout and spirituals, and it was thought to supplant them with more decorous forms of worship that were characteristic to the traditions of the white Protestants. Eventually, many black churches began to adopt the pattern of the Evangelical Protestant traditions for their youth ministry programs, which put more emphasis on individual salvation, sanctification and purity as primary life-paths.

According to some theologians, there was a considerable amount of tensions between the key components that had to do with priestly functions verses the prophetic functions and worldly verses this-worldly theologies, and, of course, some were accommodating to an attitude of resistance toward white Christianity. The black church faced an apparent struggle to teach the youth the application of Christianity, which dealt with how to practice Christianity in addition to purity. Many of the black churches were effective at including both in their youth ministries. Other problems that were in the form of support contributed to the prior dominance of the black church.

Youth Ministry in the Church of God in Christ

It would be remiss to not share the total impact of the various youth ministries and youth programs that were implemented in the Church of God in Christ. The Church of God in Christ (COGIC) is a Pentecostal Christian denomination with a predominantly African-American membership. It was founded in 1897 by the Bishop Charles Harrison Mason and is purportedly the largest black denomination in America. The denomination reports having over five million members in the United States alone and six million members worldwide.

The Auxiliaries in the Church of God in Christ that have been instrumental and continue to make a significant impact on youth, included the Sunday school, the Young People Willing Workers, better known for the acronym "YPWW," and the Young Workers Christian Council known as the "YWCC." Others include the Sunshine Band, the Youth Choir, the Purity Class, and the Sewing Circle Auxiliaries. The theme of the Sunday school in the Church of God in Christ is "A child saved is a soul saved plus a life." This resonates in the assembly of heaven and pays homage to the initial idea planted in the hearts of mankind by God to impact society through children and youth ministry and to populate heaven and the kingdom of God on earth. Their programs have been part of a foundation to shape millions of predominantly African American youth.

Some records indicate that in the COGIC, the Sunday school began in 1908 in Lexington, Mississippi, by principal L.W. Lee of the college in Natchez, Mississippi, who was also a professor. He was it seems the first superintendent of the Sunday school. True to form, most things that are going to play a critical role in the Church and be used of God come with great resistance. In 1916 in St. Louis, Missouri, the Sunday school met its resistance inside the church, and Bishop Mason was called to St. Louis when an elder, F.C. Christmas, led Sunday School with nine women and three men. After seeing the positive effects, Bishop Mason deemed that it was wholly good for the entire church.

After building the Sunday school department in every state, Bishop Mason appointed Elder Father Christmas as the international superintendent of the Sunday school in 1924. Sunday school excelled to the point that there was a national Sunday school convention in Kansas City, Missouri. The theme was coined by the Sunday school that "if you don't know your Bible, you need the Sunday school. If you know your Bible, the Sunday School needs you."

The Sunday school included classes for every age group, and many classes were combined. Children of all ages learned the Bible with the implementation of the Sunday school. Adults became knowledgeable of the Word of God and the foundational doctrines of the Church of the Lord Jesus Christ. The Sunday school (still God's design) impacted people in the church, and they learned the Bible and how to study it systematically when the quarterly Sunday school lessons were introduced. This allowed all churches to study the same lesson every Sunday of the year. The Sunday school publishing house was started in 1968 to produce the Sunday school materials in COGIC worldwide. The COGIC made history when the Sunday school was made truly international in 1999 going live on the web and was considered by many the world's greatest Sunday school session. The Bible was studied in COGIC churches on the Christian Sabbath mornings for an hour while the Young People Willing Workers (YPWW) allowed for Bible study on Sunday evenings prior to Sunday night worship services.

The YPWW was another auxiliary underneath the COGIC. It emerged as another tool to teach the youth and to lead them in a time of great social unrest and pointed the way for spiritual education, enrichment, and evangelism. It became a large training organization similar to what the Baptists call BTU or Baptist Training Union. It circumvented doctrinal dogmas that surfaced to target the youth. The biblical doctrine combated the political, racial, and explosive culture of its time. These services were very attractive to the youth, and many received the baptism of the Holy Ghost as the presence of God permeated the services.

The YPWW included training and Bible study along with the special inspirational meetings. This is what was attractive to the youth. Youth draw youth, and the YPWW, along with the other auxiliaries, created a hunger for the things of God while inspiring many youth to be saved.

The Sunshine Band also inspired many of the children. The Sunshine Band was basically a children's choir for ages up to about ten. They learned spiritual songs in addition to being taught in the Sunday school by their age groups.

Another auxiliary was the YWCC and the Purity Class. The YWCC was the "Young Women's Christian Council" which provided practical and spiritual leadership for young adult women, and the Purity Class was primarily for teenagers and adolescent women.

The youth choir provided training for the music ministry of the youth and provided great inspiration. Many ministers of music and musicians arose in the Youth Choir. Music, as in all churches, played a critical role in the ministry of the church for both adults and youth.

The Rise of the African American Middle Class

Around 1890, about ninety percent of the black population was located in the southern part of the United States in the area sometimes called "the rural black belt." However, by 1990, over eighty percent of African American churches were in the urban centers, which accounted for a huge amount of the black population, and erosion occurred in the traditional African American church.

The NAACP, along with the National Urban League, were secular institutions that were important elements that proposed legal and political solutions (verses spiritual and ecclesiastical solutions) to the problems that were unique to blacks. The movement of the black population from rural to urban settings produced the African American middle class. The rise of the African American middle class was another factor that seemed to have a diffusing effect on the membership of the black church, which initiated a type of separatist black nationalism movement. Secular careers such as law and medicine became as equally attractive as to those in the ministry, which actually birthed most of the great civil rights leaders.

Other Movements that Impacted African American Youth

Around the 1960s, many organizations such as the Student Non-Violent Committee and the Nation of Islam were the culprits that influenced the alienation of some black youth from true Christianity.

This attitude of separation and division in the black community caused them to experience a certain level of widespread growth and had some militant characteristics.

Some challenges that negatively had an impression on the black church and the ministry to the youth were greater than others. Racism showed its face in a totally new form during the emergence of the Civil Rights movement. Racism became more sophisticated and new ways were contrived to exclude or exploit African Americans. The youth were severely impacted, but now on the basis of race, but there was systemic justification based on economic and political grounds. It was very subtle, yet effective at promoting a mindset of white privilege.

One example was a project set up by the American government to open up what appeared as opportunities for blacks to serve in the Vietnam War in exchange for educational and vocational benefits that were formerly denied to black men. Eager to take advantage of the opportunities, many black men ended up serving on the front lines for the country, only to never return to take advantage of those educational benefits. Affirmative action appeared to erode when a type of supply-side economics, implemented by some Republican administrations, caused it to lose its swagger. Unfortunately, subtle forms of racism were rampant and had a devastating effect on the urban community of the blacks.

The culture of the African American youth must be understood to effectively minister to them. Unemployment was and has always been consistently higher among African Americans when compared to the rest of the population in America, and the rate is even higher among black youths. Unemployment rates were as high as forty to fifty percent in the 1980s among blacks between the ages of seventeen and thirty-five, and in some areas it was as high as eighty percent. The problem was only exacerbated by the reformation of welfare. Some reports indicated that over seventy percent of those who were removed from welfare since the year of 1996 have not found other means of income or stable employment. Many of those affected were black youth.

Teenage pregnancy has been another issue in the African American community since the American subculture embraced the sexual revolution in the sixties. Black youths account for twice the number of teenage pregnancy when compared to those of white youth. Black on black crime is an epidemic, and the statistics tell a very tragic story. Federal crime figures indicate that the leading cause of death among African American males between the ages of fifteen to thirty-four is homicide. More tragic than that is that the reports show that for almost thirty years (1967-2004), over 90% of black murder victims were killed by black offenders.[15]

The sacred and secular were considered interchangeable among this group of African American Youth during this era as school assemblies sang the songs and the church played an active role in politics and social reform for the African American youth.

The school systems in the United States have been a culprit because of educational inequalities in the black community. Schools in the black community do not have the financial support of other communities due to the lack of population that are able to pay taxes to support it. Due to the lack of funding in the tax base, the schools in the inner city lack the financial capabilities to support some of the

---

[15] www.killbobc.org

intellectual programs that are considered the norm in some suburban schools.

A final enemy among African American youth has been street crime. Many African American youth have been victims of homicide as black on black crime escalated to alarming proportions as the leading cause of death. Over half of the prison population is African Americans, and this number is even higher in some areas. Black street crime, the most widely and evident ill of the black community, is believed to be caused by the enduring poverty that has served as a catalyst to promote a sense of acute powerlessness among black youth. Where the focus on racism was primary, it was replaced with "black on black crime." Racism has submerged and become subliminal, giving way to street violence.

Youth Recruitment and Retention

Some churches are confronting the dynamic of powerlessness and empowerment with the re-emergence of Christian formations into freedom among the African-American youth. The African American youth is not alone in that they struggle, along with other church youths, to discern Christian freedoms. However, in the urban communities, it is definitely a challenge that has increased alarmingly. Some African-American churches are meeting the challenge, while others are not.

Some African-American churches are experiencing difficulty in their recruitment and the ability to retain teenagers in their churches. Some of the churches do not offer any type of youth ministry whatsoever. Some of the churches are archaic in their approach to youth ministry and are not able to relate to the youth of today. Many of the youth are not attracted because the church's ministry that is directed to them is boring and are not relevant to the times. A very small percentage of the African American churches hired youth ministers, and so their traditional non-emerging services are not attractive to youth. Many American churches have lost their appeal to the youth, and the African-American church is no exception in some cases and in other cases, they, like others, have succeeded. To perpetuate freedom of worship, expressions, and culture, the church must be open to critiquing.

One model that is proving to be effective is the kinship model. Prior youth church models encouraged the separation of youth in order to effectively minister to them. However, this model actually runs as a second church concurrently with the church that is intergenerational. This style of youth ministry, while accepted, can pose its own set of problems because it promotes a mentality that can be both divisive and create generation gaps when compared to the "we" mentality of a sense of belonging.

The kingship model centers on the inclusion of all the generations together, with communal worship that empowers the adolescents of the mainstream culture from a biblical, ecclesiastical stance. The roots of this go way back to the ancestry of the African Americans. This model involves young people in the worship life of the church and does not exclude them. Young people are actively involved in every phase of the worship, including the singing, preaching, helps ministry, and outreach. This model welcomes and embraces the youth and is instrumental in the formation of the youth in the "lay apostle" type approach.

The model has superseded the former church model of youth being involved in only the choir and singing, the junior usher board, and the young people's union. This intergenerational model has proven effective for some churches, especially in the black community, including on the issues of purity, sanctification, and social practices that accurately reflects the purpose of being unashamedly Christian and unapologetically black. Mentorship, and its ability to teach youth by hospitality, has always been an effective tool that has been used in the African American church.

Many troubled youth just need a helping hand and some guidance at critical times in their lives. Some adults have ministered to these youth by taking them in their homes and feeding them, as well as assisting with homework and becoming directly involved in every area of their lives. This has proved successful for many a youth if guidelines are set and adhered to by both the youth and the youth worker. This sort of youth ministry is nontraditional but can precipitate the turnaround of a troubled youth's life and acceptance of the Christian faith.

Youth and Musical Culture

African American youth ministry varies from church to church, but three main areas of worship should be addressed in African American Church: worship, discipleship, and evangelism.

Music has always played a key role in the African American church and has been a big emphasis for youth in the church today universally. Creative ways for youth to express their worship and devotion to God can be both inspirational and a tool for evangelism. Christian rap music is a great way to combat the violent rap music that has permeated the black culture—not for worship, but for personal music styles among youth. Stepping is a modern form of the marching band and was highly promoted in historically black colleges, but it is another style that can be used for worship that releases energy and can be a time to worship God. The traditional youth choir has always been an effective force for youth.

While many Caucasian American youth choirs are experiencing decline, they are on the rise in African American churches as a continued successful tool for worship. The most recent discovery of the liturgical dance that was even performed in Scripture has been a huge success in the African American church because it provides a visual parable for the songs they sing in worship. Expository forms of teaching the Word of God that include drama, mime, and demonstrative sermons are important to provide direction in dealing with the relevant issues that the youth are facing in this age.

Youth Discipleship and Mentoring

Another effective tool is discipleship training, which is also an element of the mentoring process, and is crucial, just as it is in any youth group. Sunday school has always been a powerful force for youth throughout time, but it is important to allow innovation in this area to keep it exciting and relevant to current times. Small groups help in the area of discipleship greatly, and they give the youth an added sense of belonging. Evangelism is important in all aspects of ministry, but for the African American youth, it is critical to reach out to the community and to the city as well. Lock-ins have shown great appeal in African American youth ministries and seemed to work great because of the overnight appeal.

Discipleship is an element of mentorship. Budget restraints that pastors and youth pastors normally have to work with make mentorship one of the toughest areas of recruitment for a youth pastor. The lifestyle of each leader and youth worker is vital to the successful communication of biblical truth. Youth pastors must firmly plan several steps if they expect to have a successful mentorship program. One thing to consider is the youth leader must narrow the scope of the mentoring plan to how, when, and what is to be expected as a mentor.

The second thing to consider is if the plan will work for that particular youth group. The youth pastor must be successful himself at mentoring youth, because a youth pastor cannot give what he himself does not have; therefore he or she must first be a successful mentor.

Thirdly, the youth pastor must be realistic and set goals that are attainable for mentoring. He or she must define the strategy of the mentoring program and what they wish to accomplish. Three of the areas in the mentoring program should be considered: friendship type mentoring, vocational type mentoring or supportive type mentoring. Once this has been established, the youth pastor must communicate effectively that vision and begin the recruitment of members to carry it out with him or her. The senior pastor, along with the congregation, will prove to be invaluable and will help determine success or failure of a mentoring program.

Adequate training must be provided to those wanting to participate in the mentoring process for the youth. Each prospective mentor should be able to pass a background check, even those from the church. A great deal of prayer should take place in the mentoring selection and in matching each youth with a mentor. Once the selections are made, whatever materials that are needed for the mentor should be provided and a support system put into place for that mentor.

Mentoring itself is not a new concept. Jesus mentored His disciples and trained them how to mentor others in the way of the Master. Many social mentoring programs have evolved with the intent to deal with the daunting task that seems to touch many African American youth at higher level than other youths.

One social mentoring program called "BEST" began in the year of 1965 as a special youth ministry program to an African-American section in a city in the Midwest. Inside a church basement with a budget of only $25,000 dollars and one staff member, BEST, which was the acronym for Building Educational Strategies for Teens, was extremely successful.

In less than thirty years, the agency grew to over three hundred and fifty active students from the ages of six through eighteen and to include fifty teenage employees. The BEST program expanded to two locations, and by the mid- nineties, they had over two hundred and fifty volunteers that participated on an annual basis in the BEST program. By this time the operating budget had grown to well over one million dollars. The program was very comprehensive and included educational, mentoring, and recreational activities. The students worked on traditional type educational subjects, but novel programs were implemented as well.

Five different scholarship programs were offered through BEST that provided college financial aid to students who graduated from high school. More than two hundred youth participated in the program, and mentors worked with the young adults from their enrollments in the program at a very young age. Many youths were able to experience their first paying jobs through the BEST program and provided job training and assisted in career searches for the youth. The BEST program included the nuclear family in the process (within certain guidelines) from the very onset of the program. BEST included the youth, the parents, as well as the staff in the decisions that it made in regards to the agency.

The format for the BEST members strongly resembled the home and family structure that many families are accustomed to. When the children and young people come to the agency after school, they usually grab something to eat and work on completing their homework assignments with their mentors; sometimes they have group planning sessions on college and activities that will be mentally stimulating and informative.

The congregation of the church initially and wholly supported BEST, but eventually financial support came from a broad – networks of corporate, governmental, foundation, and individual donors amassed. They also monitored the accountability of BEST through its board of directors. The program's director made a summary of the vision of BEST in the year of 1994 stating that the BEST program provided a setting of peace and tranquility for the youth from the chaos that was outside the steel doors of the BEST office. Such an atmosphere was conducive for religious education and the acceptance of a spiritual transformation.

Today the Bethel church has made the full circle as a birthplace of liberation for so many African American youth and the challenges they face in the twentieth century. Through church sponsorship, many programs are still implemented that includes the rites of passage program, the Teen Pep, which is a pregnancy education program, and Ezekiel's Army, a juvenile-ministry for justice whose sole purpose is to stem the tide of juvenile crime in young black men.

Agents of Change

Exogenous and endogenous are agents of change unanimously, and pressures from within the church and external to the church led to the practice of involving youth in different expressions and not just hearers of biblical theory. The ecumenical movement was a monumental change for churches in the twentieth century. The Protestant church in America joined the World Council of Churches (WCC) in the year of 1948. In pursuit behind them were the Orthodox churches, and they both formed the National Council of Churches or NCC. These organizations represented over fifty million Christians in America alone. After Vatican II, the Catholic Church did not join these organizations, but she was certainly a frequent visitor among the gathering that proceeded.

This was a revolutionary move that marked the beginning of the procedure to bury the hatchet among the denominations and become the true Church of Christ; thereby, increasing the effectiveness of the church to minister to the lost, its youth, and the world.

Chapter VIII

THE WALTHER LEAGUE

The Walther League partially includes and covers the integration of the Lutheran Church into the mainstream society of Christianity in America. The Walther League was the process and a major catalyst that assisted them as they assimilated into the culture of America. One of the primary goals of the Walther League was to develop and nurture the youth in the service and knowledge of the Christian lifestyle. In the year of 1930, O.P. Kretzmann was appointed as the executive secretary of the league, and he was responsible for its reorganization. The Lutheran church was the avenue whereby the Walther League would educate the youth and engage them in spiritual reformation. The youth were called "Leaguers" and were taught catechism and instruction all the way up through the eighth grade. The Walther league had its own publications in the form of quarterly guides, and they were used regularly for Bible study. The revelation truth of justification by faith was the central theme of the Bible studies including theology and ecclesiastical leadership. The youth meetings held by the Walther League consisted of five components including, worship, education, fellowship, service and recreation.

Immigrants from Germanic and Scandinavian countries migrated to America during the early nineteenth century. Like most other nationalities, they formed churches to perpetuate their own ethnic preferences and to practice their beliefs. The variety of Lutheran synods was so vast by the turn of the century, that it almost equaled the number of immigrants. This led to the consolidation of Lutheranism into two mainline American denominations. One was called the Lutheran-Church-Missouri Synod and the other was named the Evangelical Lutheran Church in America.

Most American Lutherans openly favored the German side of the World War I conflict. When the United States was injected into the conflict of the war against Germany, many Americans became suspicious of the Lutherans, and, as a result, persecution arose. Many of the Lutheran churches were victimized by arson and vandalism. As a response to avoid persecution in America, they assimilated more into the American society by changing their official language from German to English.

Purity vs. Practices

Recreational activities varied depending upon the particular church, however, the Lutheran were opposed to dancing. They were totally against dancing because they felt that it ignited the sexual passions of the youth. The Walther League interpreted and taught that any act or gesture including the act of dancing was sinful, and if a girl allowed a boy to dance with her, she was considered half a virgin for allowing the guy to touch her. Interestingly enough, the boy's virginity was not considered to have diminished during such an action.

The League's educators did not only teach spirituality and Bible classes, and they also addressed the natural side of things such as church etiquette and manners. The league made every effort to teach the youths, who were middle class youth for the most part, about standards of appropriate behavior such as tardiness, timeliness, not chewing gum in church, teachings against makeup in church, or make any business appointments in church. They also strongly recommended a dress code, and they did not allow shorts and certain clothing for worship. The teaching emphasized to the youth and reminded them that everything they did reflected on their reverence for God and taught them to respect the house of God. Relaxation for the youth was not to be done at church.

Outreach Ministries

Youth ministry made the transition from monasteries, convents, and Sunday schools to the modern idea of summer camps among many mainline denominations. Camps were a major form ministry outreach for the Walther League throughout the United States during the middle of the twentieth century. The camps lasted for a week, at times with the rental of the YCMA campgrounds and other campsites owned by other denominations.

The Walther League did own a few of its own camps, with the camp Arcadia in Michigan near Lake Michigan being the best property. A donor gave Camp Michigan to the league in 1922. Arcadia was considered the "international" camp that they used to train leaders in the Walther League for over forty-five years.

The director of the Walther League camp training program used the format of a military school for the camp. The dormitories were set up with the names of Army, Navy, and Cadets; there was an inn that accommodated houseguests that visited each week. The meals were served family style and were eaten in the army regiment style with a strict schedule. They even sang songs that were to the tune of "Onward Christian Soldiers." To the youth of the Walther League, God no doubt seemed very militant and stringent and was someone who needed soldiers. This military structure for the camps did change somewhat, with some of the rules easing a little bit at camp Arcadia eventually as time passed.

The league also managed to evolve its youth ministry techniques with varying forms of teaching their vision to impart "Christian knowledge" to the youth. Although Christian knowledge remained the central theme of the Walther League, it made a shift and the League became more accommodating and with openness began to experiment with social and theological changes. The camps were the exact place to implement the new ideas. Worship services began to be held twice a week, on Sundays and Wednesdays evenings, and outdoor chapel was located near the beach, which dramatically changed the atmosphere of the traditional church setting. New youth leaders were chosen based on his or her expertise in Bible theology and ethics to start the practice of two-hour lectures in large assembly halls. The Walther League youth acquired an appreciation for nature and gained respect for the new pathways that were presented to them regarding Christian knowledge due to the new innovative strategies of the Walther League.

The Walther League developed their leaders through college education by way of Valparaiso University, which was founded in 1859, but the Lutherans purchased it in 1925 from a bankruptcy. Valparaiso was one of the first Christian Universities created for the sole purpose of preparing the Lutheran youth for roles in the secular society. Many of the Lutheran youth flocked to Valparaiso when they realized that the initial leader of the Walther League had become the president of the college.

Attendance at chapel was mandatory, but was eventually replaced with theology classes and religious studies for all the students. The curriculum changed from teaching primary Lutheran dogma to classes that taught the history of Christianity and also world religions. What was once an all-Lutheran faculty has become more diversified to include Roman Catholics, Sikhs, Jews, Muslims, Buddhists, and most of the major religions in the United States. The emphasis for hiring has been placed on credentials and loyalty to the Lutheran denomination, and Valparaiso makes it clear in the employment contracts that the university is sympathetic to the Christian tradition. Postgraduate degrees are encouraged by the Christ Honors program, which sends students to the elite graduate schools in America. College is only one of the many ventures that grew out of the Christian knowledge vision.

Another venture of the Walther League was a new publication entitled *The Cresset*, which was sponsored by Valparaiso. The publication's goal was to expand the awareness from the Lutheran viewpoint to promote Christian knowledge, merging it with public life. This did cause a great deal of controversy, since many German-American Lutherans were partial to Germany, when Adolph Hitler came to power.

The editor of the publication was Reverend Walter A. Maier, and he was a professor at Concordia Seminary. He had a radio program called the "Lutheran Hour" and was known for his international speaking engagements. Many of the articles in the publication leaned toward validating the regime of Hitler and noted the reports of violence against the Jewish people in Europe as merely propaganda. *The Cresset* also offered some of the most informative critiques of the Nazi regime from the Christian viewpoint as well.

In 1938, Kretzmann reported from German radio and literary sources on the burning of synagogues and the religious persecution of the Jewish people. The report maintained that the persecution against the Jews was against all of Christianity. These articles revealed to the young Lutherans knowledge on topics that they had not been made privy to before. The articles also provided knowledge on literature, the arts, and sciences, and included social and political affairs.

The Walther League's primary publication, *The Walther League Messenger*, had a considerable reading audience because the Lutheran youth were readers. The publication changed its concentration, like many other denominational youth movements, from its emphasis on purity to emphasize practicing the Christian knowledge that was provided. Each issue of the publication continued to promote Bible study, foreign missions, and sanctification to the audience of young readers and was purely from the conservative Lutheran viewpoint.

Reverend Maier resigned as the editor due to persecution regarding his stance on anticommunism, which was reflected in an article that he had written in the publication. The new editor was Alfred, P. Klausler, and his Lutheran theological stance was more liberal. By 1948, the emphasis had shifted to social and racial equality. Near the end of the 1950's, references to personal purity and biblically prohibited lifestyles were no longer addressed in the publication.

The Walther League was instrumental in instilling Christian acts of compassion and service through several social service programs within its youth. One of the programs that ran was the hospice program. It was a mirror of the former YMCA, and its model provided shelters for young Lutherans who were making relocation changes. Room and board, unemployment services, and various hospitality programs were included. This actually helped Lutherans who were previous farmers to migrate to the city, providing assistance because of the language barriers. The hospice residences in the 1920's were actually real estate owned by the league. The St. Louis hospice was lots of fun for those who stayed in it. The women attended church, ate their meals together, studied the Bible, and sponsored social activities in the large living areas. The hospice program was discontinued during the Great Depression, and many Lutherans had entered the mainstream American culture.

The Wheat Ridge Sanitarium was another venture funded by the Walther League, founded in 1904. It was a facility that offered treatment for Lutherans who had been infected with Tuberculosis with an air treatment. Air treatment in the state of Colorado was considered a medical theory that helped to relieve the symptoms of the disease. The League borrowed an idea from the Red Cross, using it also as a fundraiser when they implemented the mailing of Christmas seals in exchange for charitable donations raising hundreds of thousands of dollars annually. The Sanitarium was incorporated as a hospital after the medical breakthrough of penicillin. The support for the Sanitarium was shifted to the Wheat Ridge Ministries, whose theme was to support and service all as a social service agency.

A new Lutheran social venture emerged at the St. Louis Amphitheatre was called the Choral Union. Youth were moved to tears as the choir sang out loudly in over six hundred and fifty voices the song, "A Mighty Fortress Is Our God." This initiated the annual public Choral Union in every Walther League convention and also on the regional and local district levels. Over nine thousand attendants gathered to hear a five hundred voice Lutheran choir perform along with the Denver Symphony Orchestra. Lutheran youth learned a lifetime of how to serve others, and the church publicly with their voices.

The league youth were also encouraged to support the military men and servicewomen. They held services for those that enlisted prior to departure. Many Leaguers enlisted in the armed services, and many Lutheran churches kept what they called "honor rolls" that listed the men and women from each church that were servicing their countries through the military. A wartime service fund was instituted by the Lutheran youth, with over one hundred twenty thousand contributions collected by the end of World War II. Christian knowledge and service is still being practiced as the central theme among the youth of the Walther League.

Youth and Missions

Fifty years after its origination, the vision of purity was no longer a priority for the Walther League, and the agenda developed to form youth without concern for purity gained steam. Acts of compassion were still greatly encouraged as foreign missions were supported with vigor. The League sent missionary builders to the foreign field to serve on various construction sites. On one particular mission field, some of the League's youth spent two years in the country of New Guinea, and in Mambisanda they helped to build a hospital, school, doctor's and nurse's residence, and other construction that was needed. Practicing the faith was the main agenda; however, purity was not.

The daunting task of moving youth from the position of complacency and passivity to a position of acting with compassion became the primary vision of the Walther League in the sixties. This was another launch of a national program that promoted the social gospel. It was based on Matthew 25:40 and called the Inasmuch Program, and it stressed practicing Christian faith over Christian purity. Tons of literature was produced to support the new agenda's focus. League members produced devotional books, Bible studies, filmstrips, tracks, and manuals for the League's districts.

The first phase of the Inasmuch Program was actually the youth work camps. The camps involved hospital visitation, actually working with doctors, nurses, and patients in hospital. There were youth work camps that transformed fearful youth into strong witnesses for the cause of Christ. Lutheran youth around the world took part in the events that encouraged servitude. The church denominations as well as youth groups sponsored the events. The servant events literally transformed thousands of youth and their leaders by practicing the faith through compassion. The Leaguers were taught to practice the faith by doing what Jesus did, and that was good.

The Demise of The Walther League

Back in 1950, it was still considered uncommon for women to preach a homily, but the Walther League allowed opportunities for women who exhibited leadership skills. This was against the advice of the leadership of the Lutheran Church. The League continued on this trend and helped to eradicate the gender roles in the church during the fifties and sixties.

The preservation of youth purity was the primary function of the Lutheran adolescents up until the nineteen fifties. Lutherans even referred to their organization as a bureau, which emphasized marital fidelity and sexual purity. However, an accommodation of violence contributed to the demise of the Walther League.

During the sixties, the nation and the churches in America experienced a division. Civil rights, the Vietnam War, and conflicts on morality caused erosion among the youth. Caught in the middle, the youth were in the very center of the conflicts that arose between those who had served the nation through patriotism and a new generation of youth who had not. The purity of the youth was a grave concern, and many critics of the League had already begun to make statements about worldliness in the League.

However, purity was not the only paramount issue of conflict. Dick Gregory, a civil rights leader, was allowed to speak at a League conference to a crowd of over five thousand young people. Gregory blamed the church in part for the problem of racism, citing that the church had failed to step forward with its leadership and influence to help in the liberation of those who were oppressed; he of course was speaking about African Americans. His speech caused a huge controversy among the League, even though Dick's invitation to speak was a consensus among League leaders and lay members.

Another reason for the demise of the Walther League was due to a controversial accusation of anti-Semitism, but it encouraged the dialogue of Lutheran and Jews to resolve the issue. Finally, many parents and Lutherans withdrew their support of the League when a folksinger was invited to sing at the League's convention in the year of 1965. Many considered Pete Seeger to be un-American and were outraged that the League would invite him to sing. The League experienced reorganization from the fallout of the convention and eventually became a youth-led, issue-oriented movement by the year of 1968.

In 1971, attendance at the convention had fallen to less than one thousand, and the financial support had begun to dry up as parents and pastors refused to allow the youth to participate in what they considered the "new Walther League" because the League's direction was corrupting the youth under the guise of Lutheranism. The Walther League was once a vibrant, emerging ministry that focused on the purity of young people and educating them in Christian knowledge. The League self-destructed as violence erupted in the American culture and the Walther Leaguers, their parents, and their leaders pulverized the movement.

Chapter IX

STRUCTURED YOUTH ORGANIZATIONS

The YMCA, which is an acronym for the Young Men's Christian Association, was founded in 1844 in London, England, by Sir George Williams with the sole purpose and intent of making an impact on young men using Christian principles. His aim was to accomplish this task by using the biblical principles to effect the spirit, soul, and body, which he believed would transform the young men since he described himself as a "careless, thoughtless, godless, swearing young fellow," (Binfield) but eventually became a devout Christian. He advocated putting into practice a system to benefit the whole man – spirit, soul and body – through development and the application of those principles.

George was a young man of only twenty-three years of age himself when he founded the YMCA. He formed it after viewing firsthand the conditions of young men being drawn from the country into the city and being thrust into the industrial revolution and the deplorable surroundings that it created for the adolescent young men. He and his colleagues had a genuine concern for the young men because taverns and brothels were a tipping point for depravity and immorality. There was a severe shortage of healthy activities that could help in the development of the character and morals of young men. His own life had been transformed by becoming a Christian, and he engineered the creation of a secure place for the young men to meet and called it the YMCA. The young men assisting him were some of his fellow countrymen who were working as drapers in the city, and they gathered other young men and began meeting with them to help circumvent the temptation and lurid lifestyles of immorality and crime that were blatantly enticing them.[16]

Explosive Growth of the YMCA

The Young Men's Christian Association (which is commonly referred to in the United States as the "Y") is now a global organization totaling over 45 million members, which consist of over 125 national federations. The Y is a voluntary association that opens its membership and services to all people, regardless of their beliefs, social class, age, or gender.

The YMCA history originated with to close to one hundred leaders of individual YMCAs from Europe and North America who gathered for the first time prior to gathering for the Paris World Exposition in 1855 to discuss the possibility of the establishment of a federation. The meeting in Paris resulted in the Paris Basis Principle, which were the guiding principles and are still considered as the themes of the YMCA today. The YMCA determined that they would respect the local autonomy of the individual YMCA societies, and the main purpose of the YMCA were reiterated.

[16] http://en.wikipedia.org/wiki/YMCA

The main purpose that inspired George Williams to found the YMCA was to unite all young male Christians to expand the Kingdom of God. The YMCA considered itself one voice in union yet maintaining independence. The motto was based on the Scripture in St. John 17:21 with the commandment of Jesus praying may "They all may be one." By the year 1851, the YMCA had expanded to the United Kingdom, Canada, the United States, Australia, Switzerland, Belgium, Germany, the Netherlands, and France. Germany held the fourth world conference in 1865. The meeting's goal also included the importance of developing the whole individual in body, mind, and spirit.

In 1878, a YMCA was established in Geneva, Switzerland, and in Norway in the year of 1880. In the Year 1885, George A. Sanford and Sumner F. Dudley established an additional YMCA location near Camp Dudley as the first in North America that was considered a residential camp. This camp relocated to New Jersey and also New York in 1891. As many Europeans migrated to America, the YMCA was instrumental in working the ports of Europe due to its connection with the World Alliance.

The twentieth century began with the YMCA as a very strong influence upon scouting, including both the Boy Scouts of America and of Germany. Throughout the twentieth century, many YMCAs were established. These include the first Indian YMCA program in 1916. In 1923, the YMCA of China piloted various projects and methods that became very popular. The YMCA was established in Jerusalem in 1928.

YMCA Wartime and Intellectual Efforts Ignited

True to its mission of ministering to young men, during World War I the YMCA was a part of the support effort as it helped to aid prisoners, providing equipment, musical instruments, art materials and other items that were needed.

"During World War I, the YMCA raised and spent over $155,000.000 to support the welfare and war efforts for American Soldiers. They deployed over 25,000 staff, military units and bases from Siberia, Egypt and France." They took over the military's morale and comfort operations Worldwide. Irving Berlin wrote a song entitled *I Can Always Find A Little Sunshine in the Y.M.C.A* in the revue Yip Yip Yaphank."

The United Nations economic and social council regaled the YMCA with a certain special status because of the World Alliance in 1947. The first African American president of the World Alliance of the YMCA was from Liberia and was selected in the year of 1955. Skin and scuba diving training was implemented in the year of 1959. Due to political unrest and major civil rights issues globally, the YMCA began to champion openly against apartheid and took a global stance for principles involving equalities, creativity and honesty and elected its first Asian president in 1985.

The initial concern of the YMCA was biblical studies, but as the YMCA grew as an institution globally, the approach to youth ministry became more holistic. Many colleges were founded due to connections to the YMCA, and they included Springfield College, Sir George University, Concordia University, Northeastern University, Franklin University (began as the YMCA School of Commerce). Michigan State University's law department classes were held at the Detroit YMCA. It seems they held a lease for almost one hundred years and upon its expiration, they moved the location to east Lansing, Michigan.

Summer schools, camps, night school, alternative programs, and day care, were all ideas that developed and stemmed from the YMCA.

Many programs that provided a ministry to youth developed and grew from their connection with the YMCA and provided a support structure to instill core values into youth such as caring, honesty, respect, and responsibility, which helped to build integrity. The core values had a color system that included red for caring, blue for honesty, and green and yellow for being responsible.

Captain Thomas Valentine was a seaman who was greatly impacted by the London YMCA and founded the first YMCA in the United States of America in Boston Massachusetts. It had the same mission statement as that YMCA with the aim to promote Evangelical Christianity by providing ministry to the spiritual, physical, and mental condition of young men. Like most YMCAs, American Ys offered educational classes, physical sports, and fitness activities.

The YMCA was blessed to become a great institution that provided ministry to the whole man in spirit, soul, and body, because it had mission statements that were in line with biblical teachings. However, the YMCA has recently dropped the "Christian" from its name and moved to just be named the "Y." The exemplarily mission of the YMCA is to be commended as it successfully shared the good news of Jesus Christ using innovative methods that forged the spiritual, intellectual and physical well-being of young men and their families, which in turn helped to create whole communities.

The YMCA advocated rights for women and children as well and worked to address poverty, dispossession, and all racially oppressed minorities, regardless of ethnicity or religion affiliation. The YMCA, along with its sister organization the YWCA, were a formidable force for Christ and its ministry to youth, children, and families.

YWCA – Young Women's Christian Association

Due to the tremendous success of the Youth Ministry for the young men, a similar program was developed to minister to the young females. Under the guise of the general female training and the prayer union, the Young Women's Christian Association or better known as the "Y.WCA", began in England just like its umbrella organization, the YMCA. The YWCA sought to be a social and spiritual support system for young English women. A social activist by the name of Lady Mary Jane Kinnaird and Christian Emma Robarts engineered this initiative program. The British empire was vast, and because of Kinnaird, the YWCA initiative expanded throughout Northern Europe, India, and the United States successfully.[17]

The YWCA played an integral part in providing educational and religious classes for young women, along with opportunities for service and recreation. As the YWCA expanded globally, the YWCA held its first world conference in 1898 in London. The principles of providing universal support for the values of service and faith globally were entrenched. The insulation of women morally and socially from urban life had been a major emphasis, but the objectives began to be modified based on the voices of thousands of working women from the United States. The YWCA began to study social and industrial issues and leaned more toward educating working women regarding legislation that would eventually impact them.

The headquarters of the World YWCA were in London up until the year of 1930, with the executive staff being primarily British, with the exception of the general secretary, who was American. The lens through which the YWCA was seen changed to Geneva, Switzerland.

---

[17] http://en.wikipedia.org/wiki/World_YWCA

The League of Nations was also located in this city, and the goal of the YWCA was to become more diversified in its associations. This move also allowed the YWCA to connect with the Red Cross and similar organizations in Geneva. The YWCA was strengthened during the World War II, even though many European countries in the East actually disbanded their YWCAs.

The relentless effort of the women of the YWCA was unstoppable as they continued to work and engage the principles of the YWCA with the construction of support systems for their neighbors and refugees. The YWCA strived to bring women together from various countries that were actual enemies during the war. The YWCA continued its work in the following decades as it worked with women on critical issues such as health, diseases, the human rights of women and girls, the advancement of women, and the eradication of poverty. The YWCA offered help with mutual services – sustainable development and the environment, education and youth, peace and disarmament, and young women's leadership. YWCAs are in over one hundred twenty countries around the world.

Great Britain has since renamed its organization name to Platform 51 in December 2010. This re-branded charity venue was made to reflect the changing attitudes and to establish its own entity but maintain its affiliations with the national and international YWCA umbrella and to better characterize the population percentage of females. The activities and services that are provided by Platform 51 offer accredited courses and information, advice, and guidance to women from disadvantaged communities. Platform 51 helps women to make informed decisions about their lives and maintain healthy relationships. The organization campaigns with them to change the lives of women in England and Wales.

For instance, the Wise Up program gives girls the ability and confidence to address MPs[18] and ministers; give TV, radio and press interviews; hold functions; and deliver group sessions. The participants develop skills in leadership, communication, teamwork, and self-motivation. In addition, the services provided for young women include informal educational, information and advice on all manner of things, courses, workshops and drop-in sessions, counseling, and one-on-one[19].

Other activities held by the YWCA that contribute to the development of young women are structured as campaigns. One such campaign that has been very successful is the "More Than One Rung Campaign." This campaign focused on helping women to get skills, to improve their financial status, and to prepare them for more opportunities to accelerate their careers. In England, this program led to the increase of the minimum wage for apprenticeships from eighty pounds a week to ninety-five pounds a week.

The Respect Young Mums campaign worked toward assisting and getting better help for teenage mothers. The YWCA championed a critical campaign chore for teenage mothers to obtain child support before pregnancy rather than after the baby is born. Effective in 2009, mothers were able to claim health in pregnancy grant from their 25th week of pregnancy. (This is similar to a pregnancy premium to income support, which was called for through Respect Young Mums campaign).[20] Due to the nature of the work done in pursuit of the development of young people, the YWCA of England and Wales is a member of The National Council for Voluntary Youth Services (NCVYS).

---

18 http://en.wikipedia.org/wiki/World_YWCA

19 http://en.wikipedia.org/wiki/World_YWCA

20 http://en.wikipedia.org/wiki/World_YWCA#1870-1930

The YWCA in the US was founded in the year 1858 and has grown to nearly 300 associations throughout the nation. The YMCA in the US has close to 1,100 locations that serve nearly three million members and participants. Recent figures show that volunteers are utilized to help with the services of the YWCA, but the YWCA does employ about 14,000 staff members, with 56% of those being part-time. The volunteer workers are the core of the YWCA's service volunteers.

In 2004, the clear majority of YWCA programs included help with children, youth, and adults, with 22% helped with domestic violence programs, 8% helped with economic empowerment and leadership development programs, 10% in racial justice programs, 7% with housing and shelter programs, 24% with child, youth and teen programs, and 24% enjoyed the benefits of health, fitness and aquatic programs[21]. The great thing about the YWCA is that it systematically advocates openly regarding critical issues such as racial justice, violence against women, early childhood education and increasing women's income issues.

The oldest YWCA is in New York and is over one hundred fifty years old. The focus of the New York YWCA is human services. The orientation considers this the most prevalent need, rather than physical services. These programs included early learning centers, family resource centers, out of school programs, and aiding in professional development and empowering programs aimed at helping women. The World YMCA states its purpose is to "develop the leadership and collective power of women and girls around the world to achieve human rights, health, security, dignity, freedom, justice and peace for all people."[22] The current YWCA sees itself as a human rights organization.

---

[21] http://en.wikipedia.org/wiki/YWCA

[22] Http://en.wikipedia.org/wiki/ywca

Christianity was the original focus of the YWCA, just like its umbrella organization. However, some chapters of the YWCA have changed their focus to social programs and services and mission-based topics.

CHAPTER X

MINISTERING TO TROUBLED YOUTH OF OUR SOCIETY

If illusions existed based on the inability to identify who the troubled youth of the twentieth century are, look no further than your own neighborhood, church, home, and family. Troubled youth come in all sizes, shapes, and colors. Youth are troubled today, and in some measures, the trouble is greater than it has been in any other time in history. America is a nation of youth in trouble, as the headlines reveal an alarming trend.

Troubled youth are young people who have problems that are more intense than that of a normal youngster and may or may not be criminal. A genuine concern about young people and the struggles they face is a concern for troubled youth. While some statistics report that juvenile crime is on the rise, others report that it is in decline. Either way, juvenile delinquents are only a portion of the troubled youth in society.

The sensationalism of juvenile crime has created fear and alarm to the point that many people are afraid of any contact with youth, not realizing that the troubled youth could be living in their household. Some statistics say that over eighty percent of America's young people under the age of eighteen have or will commit at least one offense, which they could possibly be arrested for, but a relatively small number of them are actually charged. The difference between a juvenile delinquent and a kid that is not a delinquent is being caught and not getting caught.

According to the US census reports, juveniles make up twenty one percent of all arrests.[23] Troubled youth seem to carry a stigma, and the stigma has been successful in keeping people from getting personally involved. There are some sensational cases that are horrid and very frightening, but the attitude to discuss, analyze, and over-analyze promotes mindset of, "somebody should do something." Fear, lack of knowledge of how to deal with them, and thinking somehow that it is the responsibility of others keep us from helping troubled youth.

Ministering to Troubled Youth

Fear of troubled youth is one reason we do not help them because we see them as criminals and violent. Some consider being threatened or injured by a juvenile as more scary than most people imagine. Most youth that are in trouble may or may not be situations that you know about.

Another way to define who are troubled youth are those in need of natural, physical, spiritual and emotional healing. Troubled youth

---

23

come in all forms. For example, the sixteen-year-old girl who quits school to support her family with no skills or training. The likely source of income will be illegal of some sort, such as prostitution, drugs, or stealing. Another is the kid who came to church and made a decision for Christ, yet he had been selling drugs just for survival, because he had no family to take care of him and now he is faced with the decision of what to do. Think of the young person who spends so much time at your house that he is literally part of the family and people think he is your child.

Ministering to troubled youth could be just helping a young person who has felt alienated even at church and has become a victim of their circumstances and whom the experts are expecting to write about how he or she has failed in life. Ministering to troubled youth can be very sobering, and reaching out to them can open selfish eyes and gain a new perspective for the things in life that can be taken for granted.

Ministering to troubled youth will in itself present some confrontational opportunities, but it is one of the most challenging and stubborn areas in the church, along with the need to minister to social problems and concerns. Becoming involved with troubled youth will began a roller coaster ride of frustration, satisfaction, dismay, anger, humor, joy, and sorrow. There will be many opportunities to retreat, once the decision is made to minister to troubled youth.

There are basically three areas that keep people from working with youth. First, there may be great fear of what they may do to us. Second, people feel inadequate and do not think that they are able to help the youth or they do not have skills themselves, so they wonder how they can help the youth. Third, many people do not see it as their responsibility to minister to troubled youth. Society as a whole has been guilty of ignoring troubled youth and has sometimes taken the approach of just putting them in foster homes or group homes or juvenile delinquent homes.

Some citizens are unmerciful toward youth in trouble and want them to be severely and unfairly punished. If an adult person would punish children who were sick or who were terminally ill, the law would probably consider that person to have mental problems and possibly even to be insane. Yet children who have been violated, beaten, and live in homes where drug and alcohol use is the norm are often treated with disdain and punished by society. Most of the time, school leaders, church officials, and other volunteers and church people focus on the kids that do not have issues and that are doing well. Like teachers, many of those who care for troubled youth in group homes, foster homes, and other areas are usually not compensated adequately for their services. Many of the same people that scoff at troubled kids speak out for reform for a system that they themselves are not involved in.

The people of America should observe carefully the problem of troubled youth, because no amount of money without involvement will help the troubled youth of America. The problem is on its way to spinning out of control, causing the nation untold millions of dollars. It would be wise advice to develop and reconsider a relevant ministry to troubled youth. It is only a matter of time before the neglecting of youth and children in trouble will be the biggest debt that the country has ever had to pay, and it will not only be a financial one. When youth and children in trouble are neglected, the result is delinquents, criminals, welfare recipients, and all kinds of social and mental disorders that come along with depravity. Not only is it tragic not to minister to troubled youth, but it is disobedience to God because He gave a divine mandate to minister to the children. God will hold those who do not obey responsible for what He has asked them to do regarding the children and youth, when judgment day comes, the result is not going to be nice.

Secular Ministry to Youth

Professionals can provide resources and usually have an expectation when ministering to troubled youth that sometimes gives the common person an advantage. The roles the professional must balance and are sometimes conflicting to the troubled youth because they must be willing and able to identify with the youth—which sometimes presents its own share of problems—yet provide guidance and discipline too. One example of this is a probation officer who is basically a counselor hired to provide assistance to the juvenile, but at the same time, the probation officer can recommend that the juvenile's probation be revoked. This causes a great problem with the youth, because they feel a sense of betrayal and become aloof, avoiding the professional. The person who is a non-professional has an advantage because they do not have to play dual, conflicting roles, and the youth are able to trust them and sometimes become more transparent.

Troubled youth may see the professional as someone who may be doing their job for the money and have no real genuine concern for their individual situation. In comparison, the non-professional's motive seems clearer to the troubled youth because the youth are smart enough to see that the non-professional has nothing to gain personally but the satisfaction of helping the youth in trouble. The professional can be judgmental and have the attitude of diagnosing the symptoms they see in the troubled youth, based on intellectual knowledge and expertise gained through training in their field of behavioral or social sciences. This in itself is not bad, but sometimes the professional loses sight on the person and only looks at the symptoms, making them not whole heartedly seeing the troubled youth as a person who needs help.

For example, a social worker who has a case load of fifty to one hundred kids will more than likely place their efforts on those who need the least amount of help in order to meet quotas and deadlines presented to them by their superiors. Non-professionals will not have all of these demands placed upon them and can provide quality one-on-one ministry to the youth in trouble. God can use anyone to help troubled youth, regardless of his or her skill set.

The Church's Role in Youth Leadership

When preparing to minister to troubled youth, the mindset of the ministers, the youth pastor, or the youth workers should be that it is going to be a work in progress. It will take lots of time, energy, effort, prayer, faith, and determination to meet the needs of troubled youth. The path of social responsibility for the youth is a vital tool for evangelism, counseling, and teaching. This has been a huge struggle for some churches because they feel that it does not fit into the norm of their "biblical doctrine."

The Church seems to forget that even Jesus reached out to people and met their social needs. Some examples are the feeding of the five thousand men, along with women and children, and turning water into wine for the wedding attendant who did not prepare enough for the wedding. In these examples, Jesus showed the Body of Christ that social needs are just as important as spiritual, emotional, and physical needs. In the book of Acts, deacons were appointed over the daily food distribution in the early church and were responsible for the proper care of the widows in the church (Act 6:1-7). Jesus gave a serious divine mandate to the Church: "Whatever is done for the least of those who are hungry, thirsty, naked, sick, and in prison, it is considered the same as doing for Him" (Matthew 25:40).

Troubled youth are real people with needs. The faith of the youth pastor, youth worker, and volunteer worker must be a living faith that ministers to real people with real needs. A perfect demonstration of this was when God delivered the Israelites from bondage and provided food and water for them in the desert. Jesus showed concern in the New Testament for the entire person: physical, mental, emotional, financial, and spiritual. Christians have a social responsibility as well as a spiritual responsibility. No matter how spiritual the youth pastor, evangelist, or missionary may be, they are required to minister to the whole man and not just preach the Gospel and present Christ.

Becoming involved in social needs is the requirement of every Christian and presents to the world a living, emotional, faithful, compassionate Savior who actually really cares about them. We clearly miss the heart of God and the teachings of Jesus if we take the attitude that ministry to troubled youth is not spiritual enough or that it is not as rewarding as a healing ministry, a teaching ministry, pastoring a local church, or a crusade of thousands.

Ministry to troubled youth will prove to be very challenging; however, it can bring eternal results and save the lives of the youth, if we can become the vehicle that God can drive through. We must venture outside of our comfort zone and be able to identify and relate to the troubled youth if we want to be a vehicle in which God can use to change the lives of troubled youth. Youth ministry involves being transparent enough before the kids to effectively share the Gospel to them. Stepping into youth territory takes boldness, love, and acceptance for those who may be experiencing difficulties that we are more than qualified to care for.

Innovative Strategies

What does it take to minister effectively and innovatively to troubled youth? Determining your level of preparation, values, persistence, and integrity to evaluate if you are truly ready to minister outside of your comfort zone and to think and move outside of the box for youth ministry. Heart to heart questions you must answer before preparation to minister:

(1) Are you willing to commit to a long-term relationship with the youth for maximum results? This is a time of at least a year to see a harvest come.

(2) Are you really interested in the well-being of the youth and not just willing to diagnose the symptoms of any problems they may have? Is there an underlying motive for wanting to do this?

(3) Are you ready and willing to rebound from personal setbacks and discouragements that may occur? The results may not meet your timelines and may be heart wrenching.

(4) Are you willing to immerse yourself in the youth and become involved in their personal lives and well-being, outside of the hours that are spent in church, etc.?

(5) Are you willing to ascertain if help is needed from others and other sources, to work collectively with the youth?

(6) Are you mentally and spiritually ready to deal with defeat if necessary?

Rebellion and other factors sometimes lead to unchanged youth and attitudes. Are you ready to accept the fact that your role in the youth's lives may be that of the person who waters only or plants and not the one who sees the increase?

(7) Do you realize that you will be totally dependent upon God and every resource that is made available to you will be fully utilized, yet, still in lieu of this, you will have limitations?

(8) Will you be able to do as the Bible says and judge not and not be judged yourself when you see their shortcomings?

(9) Will you be able to consider yourself during this time and your own shortcomings and past failures? Or will you minister to them with the same mercy as if it were me?

(10) Will you have the ability to empathize with the youth as if it were your own son or daughter?

(11) Are you willing to inconvenience yourself and possibly your family to minister to the youth?

The answer to these questions must be a strong, unwavering yes, because this is what will be needed and even more to grasp the daunting task of ministering to youth and to troubled youth. It has been said that ministry is work and youth ministry is still spelled the same as any other ministry – W.O.R.K.

In addition, before we can minister to others, we must be whole ourselves in our level of Christian maturity and Christian dedication. No Christian has "arrived" and is incapable of error as long as he or she is on planet earth. Youth pastors, leaders, workers and volunteers must be true to themselves. They must honestly ask themselves to question their prejudices. Adults have their own opinions and concerns and are not always able to be open and transparent.

What are the needs of the potential youth leader, pastor, evangelist, and worker? Before a leader can meet the needs of the youth, their own needs must be met. Leaders cannot impart what they do not have, and leaders cannot lead where they have never been. Moses is a great example of this truth. He was cast out from Egypt due to his eruptive act of murder and the inability to control his temper. His punishment was banishment from those he loved and was attempting to deliver. He ended up past the desert, not too far from the area where he later led the children of Israel. In other words, he knew something about the landscape that he was taking them through (although not everything).

Characteristics of Leadership

The motives of the youth leader must be pure and not be to meet his own personal needs as he ministers to the youth. What will be the goals that he wishes to accomplish by becoming involved in youth ministry? Can the love of people and a desire to see the youth fulfill their God-given destinies be readily seen as the whole purpose for this type of ministry? Are you spiritually mature and able to discern all things? The Bible says that mature Christians are able to discern right and wrong. On a scale of one through twenty, can you rate your level of maturity? Are you a doer of the Word of God and actively practicing it in your own life? The youth pastor, leader, evangelist or worker must be mature enough to allow the youth to grow without compromising their own growth and spiritual maturity.

The effective youth leader must not be a novice in his or her knowledge of the Word of God and should be able to provide sound direction that is based solely on Scripture. The effective youth leader must be courageous, although not presumptuous, with the ability to make good decisions that are right and have the fortitude to withstand opposition and unpopularity. They must be available to the youth and willing to get involved with them. They must be able to prioritize and follow orders. They must be kind, full of humility, and possess an attitude that is not judgmental. The leaders must have true compassion, kindness, humility, and a genuine care for people.

The leader must be honest and consistent; he or she must be faithful. Inconsistency is an issue that troubled youth have been victims of. Therefore, it is imperative that the leader or worker who ministers to trouble youth be consistent in their lifestyle.

The leader needs to operate in spiritual discernment in order to identify certain characteristics of troubled youth but also have the ability to help. Troubled youth are young people who usually mistrust other people, and it is usually for valid reasons. They lack significant adult supervision, direction, concern, and examples to allow them to model behavior that would be positively rewarding. They usually turn to their peers for acceptance, especially when there is not acceptance from adults. Troubled youth live for the present and are looking for instant gratification. Troubled youth usually exhibit common behavior, even unconsciously.

The attitudes of troubled youth may or may not be reflective of the lack of guidance from adult role models. Troubled youth are selfish to the extent that they are focused inward and believe that the universe revolves around them. They find some level of satisfaction in delinquent behavior, and it is basically because they are hurting inside and want to attract attention to themselves. Troubled youth are sometimes less affected by guilt, because their environment has taught them that certain attitudes and practices are normal. Therefore, their gauge of what is right and wrong is sometimes totally incorrect because they have been exposed to a set of values that are wrong. Troubled youth respond to survival instincts and how to manipulate other people for their own gain. Troubled youth do not respect the law and have a problem with authority. These are some of the things that the youth leader needs to be cognizant of when they are ministering to troubled youth.

Biblical Order for the Family

Society has implemented laws to redefine the family unit, but it is still the foundation of society. Just like when an earthquake occurs, when the foundation is cracked or broken, the building crashes down. When the structural foundation of a family is broken through various events and life struggles, this causes an earthquake in the life of troubled youth. Most troubled youth have experienced a family dilemma of some kind, and it breeds contempt.

Family crises are nothing new and have existed since the beginning of time. However, there is a familiar trait that has effected most troubled youth. Many parents are the root cause of troubled youth. The parent or parents who are unstable, unreliable, and ineffective perpetuate insecurity in troubled youth. They may or may not realize that their vacillating behavior communicates confusion and rejection to their children and to their youth.

The culture today and our fast-paced living styles have put family at the bottom of the priority list. Money, achieving recognition, and other personal and civic duties have usurped the priority of the family. The family structure is a nucleus, and that nucleus is the environment where the youth can function properly. It is a fallacy to assume that troubled youth are those youths from broken homes. Many troubled youth come from two-parent homes where there is constant violence, drug abuse, and alcoholism. Many troubled youth are inside the Church, yet the Church has not been very efficient in ministering to them. The most influential person in a young person's life is initially their parents or guardian. Youth that have strong relationships with their parents have a better chance at avoiding the tendency to fall into the ever-increasing and alarming statistical category of juvenile delinquency. The most important ingredient in a family is love.

Chapter XI

YOUTH MINISTRY STRATEGIES FOR YEAR 2000 AND BEYOND

Seventy years have passed since the American adolescents came to experience the transitional period of rites of passage and lack of social status or rank. They also remained anonymous, showing obedience and humility, submitting to forms of conduct and dress. This long liminality has contributed to purity, and the development of employees in the world's economy in recent history. However, the questions remain such as, "How has the task of youth ministry changed?" "What can the church do in this millennium to encourage and develop young Christians?" "Does the knowledge of the history of youth ministry of the past relate and equate with youth ministry today?"

The Evolution of Youth Groups

All youth ministries, African American included, were influenced by Christian tradition; however, they had different degrees of that tradition. American Christian youth were not ignorant, working for knowledge and service as they became lay apostles, witnesses, and champions for freedom on every frontier when they followed ministries that were set aflame. Therefore, youth ministry for the twenty-first century must set ablaze the path of Christianity that has been made available to them by simple cultivation.

A very real threat and impending danger is the contemporary culture of today that challenges biblical standards and values. Christian youth ministry must oppose its objection to anti-intellectualism. The Scriptures say that iron sharpens iron, and when Christians struggle together to confront the vigilant dangers of those who deliberately and blatantly oppose biblical Christian traditions, that unity will produce strength. As much as young people embrace liberation theology, and as much as women desired and wanted a feminist theology, youth in America need a new vision of the Christ. Like any other group who has been marginalized and their rights violated, youth ministers, pastors and lay people need to rethink the Christian traditions for the twenty first century and how they pertain to these marginalized youth.

Time is of the essence, and the windows of truth need to be revealed, imparting information for youth to answer firmly and confidently the questions regarding the faith and on the practices of the faith. Young people need to be able to answer with their own strong convictions, be resolute, and not be shielded from the moral debate that confronts them. As new movements are engineered, purity should be revived and not withheld from movements designed to teach young people how to put their faith in action. As the youth launch out into new horizons, they must be trained and prepared to play a role in the new millennium.

In order to effectively develop a strategy to combat the incorrect rites of passage since the 1960s, emerging youth ministries must listen to young people and observe their behavior. Youth ministries will not provide answers to youth with verbiage that only encourages them to "just say no." They cannot say no without an intimate relationship with Christ and the restraining power of God inside of them to help. Sanctification, which is separation for Christian for youth as well, is not only about negative relationships; it includes the daring boldness to detach and sanctify themselves from the violent inventions and conventions of the American culture that are blatant enemies to Christianity. Emerging youth ministries do not steal the youth to initiate them into a private class or ceremony, but they carefully plan and teach the unique use of the rites of passage.

The Need for the Emergence of Youth Pastor

According to the CDC and statistics in the year 2009, around 410,000 teenage girls gave birth in the United States. The figure represents a 37% decrease from the exploding teen birth rate in the year 1991.[24] The percentage was at 61% for every 1,000 females.[25] According to the United Nations, the United States' rate of teen pregnancy is nine times greater than those in other developed countries. According to the CDC, that means that one of every ten new mothers is a teenager showing that each day over 1,100 girls are still becoming teenage moms.

24

25 http://www.wivb.com/dpps/health/healthy_living/teen-pregnancy-rate-lowest-in-2-decades_3766282

The Vital Signs report looked at data from 1991 to 2009, and the results showed a decrease in the percentage of high school students having sex. More and more teens are using contraceptives.[26] Major drops in the teen birth statistics only mask the greater problem of abortion among teens. Abortions are easily accessible for teens, and some states no longer require parental consent for teenagers to obtain abortions. The very foundation of society is being shaken, and there are some very aggressive attempts to destroy those very foundations that begin with youth and the family structure.

America and the whole world are in a culture war to accept the unacceptable that is being shoved down the throats of the minds of people. Some of those things are the recent laws passed against traditional marriage, which was designed by God alone, and the propaganda championing immorality, which is a diabolical scheme to destroy the family and the foundations that are established by God Himself.

The world itself is in a day of great deception. The educational system, which was supposed to influence our children in a positive manner, has yielded to political correctness and secular humanism, embracing deception by slowly allowing the teachings of sexual immorality of every kind to be presented as normal and acceptable. One school in the state of Michigan plans to include a video on "coming out" in their sex education classes.[27] We are in the time period of the apostate church where denominations have begun to say that a lifestyle that caused God to destroy Sodom and Gomorrah and the cities of plain is a "gift of God." According to a magazine, the *Christian Post,* "The Central Methodist church in Ohio spread throughout their community via digital media that 'being gay is a gift

---

[26] http://www.positive.org/Resources/consent.html

from God'"[28]. The schools and some denominational churches as well as television programs have totally abandoned what the Word of God has never changed its stand on.

Every nation in its history that embraced immorality has eventually crumbled, and we have Rome to use as our perfect example. Immorality is being taught in some of the schools and some of the churches, where will the youth of today learn the truth about morality and immorality and sex as God intended (if they fail to get it at home or from a biblical church). The message of the Gospel has not changed, even to the youths. God is just as serious as He was in the beginning regarding immorality and holiness. As far as God is concerned, nothing has changed in that aspect. The youth minister of the twenty first century will face these challenges as he devises a plan to minister to youth.

Disturbing patterns in youth ministry encourage us to review our strategies of what actually is effective in youth ministry in the twenty-first century. While some American youth have been left alone as vultures drawn to violence, the Church has provided some youth ministries with countless commodities and programs. The church has failed, to a certain degree, by not communicating and demonstrating examples of non-violent and compelling depths of spiritual intimacy.

Concerning the future of youth ministry, the broad question that remains is, "Will youth ministry have the ability to emerge impactful in the millennium?" The move from purity to practice was vital in

---

[27] http://www.wzzm13.com/news/article/164702/14/School-may-add-alternative-lifestyles-to-sex-ed-class

[28] http://www.christianpost.com/news/church-touts-homosexuality-as-a-gift-not-a-sin-50010/

prior movements, but the process of purity has to be regained. Youth pastors and leaders cannot hide from reality and must come to grips with the faces of danger that are apparent in youth ministry if it fails to emerge. We must recognize the need for churches to reignite the rites of passage for the youth of the twenty first century.

Youth are faced with the rites of immorality, sex, drugs, demeaning music, and violence on an epic, unparalleled scale. Youth ministry must continue to evolve and offer today's youth an authentic intimacy in their relationships with the Church and the potential of that relationship with God. Youth ministry must embrace technology and apply practical teaching against violence. During the sixties, principles were reintroduced that were very relative to identifying purity. There is a moral cry from our youth that tells us the principles of purity must be reapplied and taught with a forceful conviction. The reintroduction of these timeless principles is critical, and the Church must identify holy living and purity as the answer.

Youth ministry is considered a very dangerous calling today by some measures. However, the danger of a generation without spiritual knowledge of God is even more tragic and dangerous. Christian youth of today have struggled since the sexual revolution of the sixties to receive some affirmation from the church as spirits with bodies that were somewhat out of control in need of relevant answers. Youth are some of the first people to recognize hypocrisy, while acting out that hypocrisy in ways that are becoming more dangerous. The Church has taken note of this and has begun to incorporate youth through diversity and the theology in application that is both more practical and spiritual.

The need is apparent; the task is daunting, dangerous, and compelling. Christian youth ministries must employ every resource to demonstrate to young people how to live. There is a simple question that is asked in youth ministries today, and that question has become a cliché: "What would Jesus do?" Youth ministry is not for cowards. To be the most effective youth minister in the twenty first century, vulnerability and courage are a must, and they must have a mindset of openness and thinking out of the box. Youth ministry must not become attached to conventional means of church and culture to reach the youth of the twenty first century.

Effective Youth Pastoring Techniques Defined

According to the Bible, the foundation for youth ministry is teaching, with the intent and purpose to seek and save the lost and to die to oneself. The youth minister must accept the critical, urgent task of imparting to the youth, in a genuine way, the incarnate presence of God for and to the youth. Youth are well aware of the dangers that seek to grasp and overtake them on a daily basis. Youth ministers who can impart and reveal the presence of God to the youth, represent the very presence of God and a real person that is willing to go the distance with them through whatever they may face.

However, the youth minister should be careful to avoid the messiah complex and become a hindrance to the youth experiencing a personal savior individually and intimately. In order to make Christ known to the youth through a living example and the greatest commandment, the youth minister must thoroughly embrace the church, the vision of the senior pastor, and the Chief Shepherd. The problem is that some senior pastors have no vision for the youth, and they are trapped in a time warp, refusing to allow the Lord to expand their vision to affect the youth in their church. When the senior pastor is unwilling or unyielding to the voice of the Holy Spirit in this area, much prayer is needed for the senior pastor and the youth pastor, as it can cause an ungodly split in the vision of that local church.

Qualifications of the Youth Pastor

The qualifications for youth ministers and leaders are still the same as any other qualification for ministry in 1 Timothy when the Holy Spirit spoke to the church through the Apostle Paul. He encouraged the young Pastor Timothy to flee youthful lust. There is a certain level of lust that will present itself to the youth, and with all the information available to the youth, the Holy Spirit spoke it to Paul to write for the 21st century. The Apostle Paul commanded the young Pastor Timothy to be an example for believers in spirit, word, manner of life, faith and love, and in his manner of living.

For the youth leader to impart values to the youth that are consistent with the Word of God, he or she must have those values, along with a level of transparency. Those values have to be demonstrated to the youth in the ministry in order for the youth to see and understand a living example of those values. Other people's lives and souls are at stake; they are on the youth minister's shoulders. So much so that if that one should fall by the way side, the minister of the youth will have to stand before God and give an account of what happened. Responsibility of a parent's child, youth, and adolescents is, in part, on the heart and shoulders of the person that is in authority. They have a God-given right and authority to live a lifestyle that matches the lifestyle that they are preaching and teaching to the youth. If one contradicts the other—or perhaps there is a disagreement between the two—an account to God will be in order, and the falling away of the youth will take place as well.

So many times people believe that the youth minister has to have some type of youth characteristics or views. The youth minister must place absolute authority in the view of the Bible, but aspire to communicate that innovatively, making it transferable and effective to the current generation. It would seem as if they would have to have been caught up with the latest status quo, music, etc. That is not the case today. However, what we do see is that the youth minister must be able to have some ability to relate to the youth. Grasping this understanding, he or she is better equipped to handle the current situations and circumstances that the children of this world face today, with full knowledge that the times have changed and evil men and seducers are getting worse.

We are nearing an apocalyptic precipice and departure from the Judeo-Christian roots at an alarming rate. This information is so key because what he or she will have to understand is that it is not about a new trick, devil, or demon that has come upon the youth; it is just a new tactic, way, or avenue by which the enemy has twisted a new look to take advantage of the kids and their souls. The youth minister must be spiritual enough for the Holy Spirit to alert him or her to these tactics, schemes, and avenues. This discernment will only come through much time spent in the Word of God and in prayer.

The only thing new is that he has used the same trick in a different format since the age of technology, and ultimate communication between anyone, anywhere, at any point in time. The enemy has used this new wave of technology with an old trick he learned back the book of Genesis. Instead of just coming out and talking to Eve and deceiving her via plain face to face talk, now in the twenty first century, this same trick can be implemented, and has been, by way of text messages, Facebook, Twitter, My-Space, messages, and all sorts of mass and social media. The knowledge explosion and technological advancements were created for the basic good of mankind but are also used as a tool to permeate evil between youths in different geographical locations in order to get them to do something that is detrimental.

The youth minister cannot be stuck and swamped in the stone ages, always saying, "back in my day…" The truth is that we are not back in that day, and that day is gone forever. The youth minister must utilize every legitimate spiritual and natural weapon to their advantage while making sure to evade any pitfalls that will definitely be presented to prevent the transformation of the lives of the youth.

The power of a unified youth worker and youth group team has the essentials to create a live, holy atmosphere. If the youth minister can keep his group synchronously connected and linked up in one accord, it is an inspiration when the youth see a youth team, including the youth minister, in one accord, saying the same thing, and following the same vision. If the importance of prayer is established and executed on a consistent and regular basis, with the youth and sometimes without, there is nothing that can stand against the youth workers and their youth minister. Unity was a key ingredient that caused the Gospel to spread to other nations as the early church experienced an explosion of growth that caused the world to be turned upside down for the cause of Christ.

Chapter XII

ONSLAUGHT AGAINST THE YOUTH OF THIS GENERATION

The Prophet Daniel saw things that would only be revealed when the end of time was near. His words, breathed by the Holy Spirit, said, "But you, Daniel, shut up the words, and seal the book until the time of the end; many shall run to and fro, and knowledge shall increase."[29]

We are the generation that has experienced the explosion of knowledge. Knowledge without God creates intellectual idiots and a society of godless intellectuals. Technology itself it seems has spear-headed the knowledge explosion. Wickedness has increased, it seems, almost in parallel to the amount of knowledge that has exploded. Technology has a purpose, and that eternal purpose is for the sake of the Gospel. Television and the Internet have been tools that have begun to escalate as instruments for the Gospel message.

---

[29] The Chronological Study Bible, New Kings James Version. Thomas Nelson 2008 Daniel 12:4.

Television, like most technology, is being perverted for the use of filth and immorality of the worse kind. The generation that grew up on cable TV has had their spirits and minds bombarded with a lifestyle and morals that are totally against the Word of God. The moral landslide that occurred in the towns of Sodom and Gomorrah and in the days of Noah is no longer coming, it has arrived on the scene for the twenty first century and is descending further into the reprobation and seems to be taking a generation captive with it.

The Bible spoke of how Lot's soul was vexed night and day by the things he heard and saw in Sodom. Cable TV and network television seem to be on a path to destroy the minds of this generation with base morals and living standards. Pornography is rampant on TV and on the Internet, with triple-X-rated movies that are shown on TV after midnight. Cable TV itself is like a needle pushing heroin into the minds and hearts of our youth of today. Many adults have been swept away with the landslide. Many Christians without a prayer life have not been able to hold on to righteousness and are drowning in a sea of filth. Unfortunately, these films feature total nudity, sexual immorality of all kinds.. Many newsstands feature explicit magazines that make Playboy look like a nursery rhyme.

Demon spirits are being imparted to children through the television media. Youth sexual crimes are on the rise, and some teenagers have become slaves to sexual sin, while being targets for incest, rape, and lewd lifestyles, as well as human trafficking.

The Bible has forewarned us, stating that seducers and evil men shall continue on a downward spiral toward the precipice of no return. Seducers, pornographers, and evil-minded men used as instruments of Satan have shown little regard for the law while entrapping innocent young children and youth with perversion and prostitution at a young age. There are reports of kids of elementary age being sold in the United States and other countries for sex trafficking. Sex education is in the school classrooms and is being pushed to portray every form of immorality as normal. Immorality is a critical issue among our youth of today, and the Bible predicts that in the last days children will be unthankful, unholy, and disobedient to their parents.

Spiritual hunger along with inconsistent unconditional love is at the root of the problem of rebellion among youth. Youth of today do not want to be told how much you care; they want to be shown the love of Jesus by their parents, those that are in authority, and mostly by those in the true Church. Apocalyptic events are occurring at a rapid pace like the birth pains that Jesus spoke about in the twenty-fourth chapter of Matthew. Spiritual guidance is imperative for youths of today, and it must begin with the children. This is one phase of the love of many waxing cold. Discipline, not child abuse, and the Word of God, when applied early and consistently enough with prayer, will drive out rebellion.

Chapter XIII

CONCLUSION

The Sunday school was a supernatural phenomenon that God used to instruct children, youth, and adults. It was also instrumental for centuries in the development of Christian character in both the youth and adults. The twentieth century brought new ideas and strategies to minister to youth. Major factors such as the Catholic Church, the Lutheran Church, the African American churches, and powerful youth movements spearheaded by individuals such as the evangelist Billy Graham brought fresh insights and inspiring programs and services to reach out continually to the youth. Structured youth programs are still in existence today such as the YMCA and the YWCA programs. Many Bible schools began to emphasize training a generation of leaders to further impact the youth as the need for youth pastors sprung up all over North America and globally. As youth ministry evolved, divine strategies have never ceased to be offered to equip leaders to impact the harvest and the youth in the end time generation.

Youth crime, teen pregnancy, the Internet, drug wars, pornography, sexual abuse, the occult, and attacks on the family structure provide great challenges for those who would take on the daunting challenge of ministering to the youth of today. Those who would accept the challenge must never forget that these challenges are not new. It was the plan of the Creator to minister to the children and the youth; the same Creator will provide strategies and innovative techniques to penetrate future generations of youth.

The Bible has given us a promise in the second chapter of Joel that indicates God will pour out His Spirit on all flesh in the last days. The Scriptures indicate that young men and young women, children, and youth are not exempt. The Master has provided every weapon and tool for maximum results. Technology, along with supernatural weapons with a pure heart of love, must be obtained and used to impact the present generation. Youth pastors, leaders and helpers of today as well as parents must contend for the opportunity to transform a generation by the powerful, innovative Word of God and all that is provided in this age of the knowledge explosion.

The youth of today are hurting, but they are also hungry for the manifestations of the Sons of God." Harry Potter, X-Men, and Avatar are not the answer for our youth today; their hope is in the preached Word of God through the dunamis power of God by the Holy Spirit that gives great witness to the resurrection of a risen Christ. The demonstration of God's tangible, visible, and undeniable power would quench their hunger and thirst for the supernatural and will reveal a true and living God and a personal Savior to them in this generation.

The biblical principles behind previous movements that were a forceful impact on the youth of the past and some youth of today are not at all without merit. However, we must venture out and not remain in the past, using antiquated techniques for youth ministry. We must earnestly contend for the power and faith that was once delivered to the saints to communicate effectively a relevant Gospel message to the youth. Whatever avenue is available must be used with a sense of urgency, and youth must be literally bathed in prayer to produce dynamic results that will be everlasting and life changing. Strategies that are used without the biblical foundations and a definite divine strategy will produce futility and disappointment, but when we apply the principles in the Word to instruct the children will reap a harvest of generations of youth.

Bibliography and Works Cited

A Cyclopedia of Education, Volume 3. Paul Monroe, Ph.D. The MacMillian Company. New York. 1911. Norwood Press.

http://www.christianitytoday.com/ch/asktheexpert/whendidsun-dayschoolstart.html

Amplified Bible. Zondervan Corporation, Grand Rapids, Michigan. 1995.

http://en.wikipedia.org/wiki/Arminianis

http://www.believersweb.org/view.cfm?ID=143

http://Bibleresources.americanBible.org/Bible-resources/Bible-resource-center/about-the-Bible/Bible -history/education-ancient-Israel.

http://www.christianhistorytimeline.com/GLIMPSEF/Glimpses/glmps163.shtml

http://en.wikipedia.org/wiki/Colonial_history_of_the_United_States

http://en.wikipedia.org/wiki/Constantine_I_and_Christianity

http://en.wikipedia.org/wiki/History_of_the_Catholic_Church

http://en.wikipedia.org/wiki/History_of_education_in_ancient_Israel_and_Judah

http://en.wikipedia.org/wiki/History_of_the_Jews_in_Ireland

http://en.wikipedia.org/wiki/History_of_the_Jews_in_Italy

Wardie, Grace Addiel. *History of the Sunday school Movement* in the Methodist Episcopal Church. The Book Concern. New York, Cincinnati

http://en.allexperts.com/e/i/in/industrial_revolution.htm

http://www.jpusa.org/lessons6.html

Wardie, Grace, Addie. The Methodist Book Concern. New York, Cincinnati.

http://ministry-to-children.com/history-of-sunday-school

http://en.wikipedia.org/wiki/Second_Vatican_Council

Brown, Marianna C. *Sunday School Movements in America.* New York, Chicago, Toronto. Fleming H. Revell Company, 1901

http://www.newadvent.org/cathen/13554b.htm (religious education in children before early BC.

Power, Caroll, John. *The Rise and Progress of the Sunday School.* Robert, Raikes and William Fox. New York. Sheldon and Company, 1863.

http://www.gracemagazine.org.uk/articles/historical/raikes.htm

http://en.wikipedia.org/wiki/Robert_Raikes

http://en.allexperts.com/e/y/yo/youth_ministry_(evangelical).htm#hd1(change

http://youthministryinstitute.org/resources

About the Author

Dr. Pamela McNeese received both her Masters in Theology and a Doctorate of Theology&Research from Midwest Seminary. She is a teacher, author, community prayer coordinator and part-time Bible School Instructor. She is an ordained Minister of the Gospel through RHEMA Ministerial Association International and she has ministered in the inner city Youth Crusades, Churches, Outreaches, and Conferences as well as the Youth Pastor setting.